JOURNEY TO EXCELLENCE

BY

Stephen S. J. Hall

First published by Dog Ear Publishing
4010 W. 86th Street, Ste H
Indianapolis, IN 46268
www.dogearpublishing.net

ISBN: 978-160844-383-3

This book is printed on acid-free paper.

Printed in the United States of America

Dedicated to

My stepfather who gave me direction
The School of Hotel Administration at Cornell
that gave me knowledge

My wife, Marge, who gives me love
and
Our children, Donna, Larry, Tom and Peggy
who give me pride

"In today's increasingly complex and global service environment, excellence is often an elusive goal. Stephen Hall provides direction by proposing that excellence is every employee's responsibility, and that it can be achieved by focusing on the dual challenges of quality and ethics. His ideas are clear, innovative, and timely. He has written a book that will be of great value to all hospitality professionals as they strive to act with integrity and consistency, and as they work together to meet the high standards they set for themselves. This book is relevant to industry practitioners and hospitality management students alike, as it highlights the role ethical practice plays in creating successful organizations."

Michael D. Johnson, Dean
E.M. Statler Professor
School of Hotel Administration
Cornell University

"The "Journey to Excellence" achieves Steve's objective — to provide a book on excellence with factual, easy-to-absorb principals that can be effectively applied with meaningful results. I thoroughly enjoyed this journey as it reinforced my commitment to excellence. I know you will enjoy it too."

Joseph A. McInerney
President & CEO
American Hotel & Lodging Association

The goal for Journey to Excellence was to produce a short, easy to read, analysis of elements necessary to achieve excellence in hospitality. The book contains 4 concepts that are new to the process. First is the concept that Quality Assurance (conformance to standards) is insufficient as a goal for excellence in that it ignores the level of standards being sought. Excellence requires conformance to right standards thus introducing ethics to the process. Second, the concept of ethics has always been difficult for managers to internalize because the definition of ethics has been elusive. Journey to Excellence proposes a simple definition that can be understood and utilized at every level. The third concept presents excellence as most successful if developed and implemented in house without large expenditures for outside expertise. Last is the concept that the process must be understood at every level of the organization. Thus Journey to Excellence is written to be read by enlightened production level employees, supervisors, Department heads as well as Senior Management.

TABLE OF CONTENTS

Foreword

I have known Stephen S. J. Hall since the early '60s, so I know firsthand that he has always been extremely logical and committed to the highest standards. As a United States Marine Officer, a successful hotel executive, an administrator at one of the world's foremost educational institutions, and a minister, his commonsense rather than emotional approach to the "Journey to Excellence" is a reflection of his life.

The book provides basic information on quality, ethics, and excellence from the supervisory to executive levels, stressing the need to not just set standards, but to consistently meet the right standards, and the ramifications of not getting it right. From E. M. Statler to J. Willard Marriott, our industry has a long history of putting the customer first and practicing ethics at every level.

Steve walks the reader through a very clear-cut "Journey of Excellence" that stresses the fact that if you want employees to meet your expectations, it starts with treating employees as if they can meet your expectations. His unification of excellence and ethics, knowing what is right and having the will to do it, should be required reading for students, executives, and everyone in between.

Journey to Excellence achieves Steve's objective—to provide a book on excellence with factual, easy-to-absorb principals that can be effectively applied with meaningful results. I thoroughly enjoyed this journey, as it reinforced my commitment to excellence. I know you will enjoy it too.

Joseph A. McInerney
President & CEO
American Hotel & Lodging Association

"Hospitality professionals embark on many journeys, but the most challenging of these is navigating the path to excellence. Stephen Hall has provided a clear and thought-provoking road map in his highly engaging book as he leads readers through the uncertainties of ethical decision making and the dilemmas of establishing and maintaining service quality. His dynamic model suggests that performance goals continuously evolve and that excellence is achieved when employees collectively hold themselves to the highest ethical standards. Journey to Excellence is an invaluable resource in guiding service employees and their organizations into the future."

Judi Brownell, Professor & Dean of Students
School of Hotel Administration
Cornell University

INTRODUCTION

My working career in Hospitality Management began in 1958 when I joined Sheraton Corporation after earning my BS degree from the School of Hotel Administration at Cornell University and serving two years as a Marine Corps Officer. I was headquartered in the home office of Sheraton in Boston and began my career in the Engineering Department. After holding a variety of positions from Project Manager, Divisional Engineer, and Engineering Cost Control, I was sent to Michigan State University in 1965 to earn my MBA, returning in 1966 to become Director of Development in what had then become ITT-Sheraton. Soon thereafter, I was named Director of Operations Support for ITT Sheraton International. Of the nine departments under my leadership, one was Director of Quality Assurance, where I worked under the direction of Phillip Crosby, the Director of Quality for ITT International. Crosby, a prolific writer and excellent speaker and a man in the Quality Assurance (QA) circle of such giants as Edward Deming and Joseph Juran, was the one who inspired me to concentrate on Quality for the hospitality industry. In 1990, I published ***Quality Assurance in the Hospitality Industry*** (ASQC Quality Press, Milwaukee, WI, 53203). The book was unique in that it was the first to specifically address quality in hospitality. Since then, the Service and Tourism field has been inundated by "how to" books and the industry has tended to pursue paths that generally promote magic-button solutions rather than basic logic. This book differs from the first in four major areas.

First, the idea that quality is simply "conformance to standards" in its many forms is misleading. Total conformance to bad standards meets the consistency test but cannot be regarded as achieving true quality. Meeting right standards is what is required, and this introduces ethics. I prefer to replace "quality" with "excellence," defined as "consistently meeting right standards."

Second, ethics, fine-tuned over the centuries by philosophers, has become too complex for everyday application and too important to be ignored. I have removed "higher-power" elements from the definition of ethics and simplified it in terms of property ownership. I believe my definition of ethics, although philosophically simplistic, is far more applicable to the service industry.

Third, the search for the quality "magic button," and the proliferation of experts helping to find it for a price, takes the focus off "in-house" everyday excellence. Although it is not hard to achieve excellence "in-house," dedication and focus are required, something many managers have tended to forget. My hero in the quest for excellence is Ellsworth Milton Statler, who was the master of service and related standards. Here is what Statler said his employees should do in their approach to service:

1. To treat our patrons and fellow employees in an interested, helpful, and gracious manner, as we would want to be treated if positions were reversed;
2. To judge fairly–to know both sides before taking action;
3. To learn and practice self-control;
4. To keep our properties—buildings and equipment—in excellent condition at all times;
5. To know our job and to become skillful in its performance;
6. To acquire the habit of advance planning;
7. To do our duties promptly; and
8. To satisfy all patrons or to take them to our superior.

Behind these admonitions was a family of standards that Statler management rigorously enforced. Attention to detail, along with outstanding innovative elements, caused E. M. Statler to be named, in 1950, 22 years after his death, "Hotelier of the Half Century." Statler did not have outside experts to tell him what to do; he had only his passion for the industry and the will to succeed. He did it "in house," and it can still be done that way today.

The fourth major difference in this book is that time is a precious commodity in today's fast world. My intent is to write a little book with a big message, one that can be meaningful for the enlightened entrance level employee to the chain executives.

I sought to write an easy-to-read book, based on logic and fact, which tells the story of excellence simply and objectively. The reader will decide whether or not I have succeeded.

Having thus spoken, I wish you bon voyage on your journey to excellence.

Stephen S. J. Hall

1

THE JOURNEY BEGINS

Recently, when I was discussing this book with some college professors at a major university, they were adamant in advising that I use some other word than "excellence." "It has been overworked to the point that it has lost its impact," they said. To a certain extent, they are correct. The word has been overused and is now thrown around endlessly. The fact is that excellence has little real meaning these days. Everybody seeks it, and most believe they practice it to perfection. At least that is what business wants you to believe; yet most practitioners misunderstand the word and the concepts it represents.

The objective of this book is to change the way we view and practice excellence. I want to restore excellence to its rightful place as an absolute necessity for a successful business. Achieving excellence is a process of doing many simple, uncomplicated things very well. Our approach is to discuss these "things" in easy, simple terms, one by one, such that the book is an easy read and, when the reader is finished, the individual concepts will be ingrained in the reader's mind. If I can make you, the reader, a true believer in the individual concepts and principles of excellence, implementation will be easy. If, on the other hand, you do not buy into the principles of excellence, I would advise you to not begin a program, because it will surely fail.

A final note: I believe strongly in the use of logic rather than emotion to make my points acceptable. The reader has to buy into this logic or else determine that my point is illogical and deny it. So I urge readers to thoroughly question every point and in Socratic fashion, ask "why, why, why?" Don't accept anything if you have the slightest doubt about its veracity. But, absent real doubt, make these principles a permanent part of your life.

Every element of the process of achieving excellence can be defended by the application of logic.

QUALITY

2

DEFINING QUALITY

Excellence begins with quality, and quality begins with a clear, simple working definition. When I lecture on the subject of quality, I begin by asking participants if they accept quality as an inseparable part of their being. The response is universally "yes." But when I follow by asking them to define quality, I receive a bunch of blank stares followed by a wide variety of answers, most of which are unworkable. For example, many define quality as performing in an outstanding manner. But they cannot define "outstanding." Some define it as excellent service. I argue that an overcooked, tough steak, served impeccably by a waiter with a tuxedo and spotless white gloves would not cause that meal to be considered quality. Consumers rate quality on the basis of the complete package received; product, service, function, and cost, not just on part of the package. At one seminar, a manager defined quality as "no ring left in the bathtub!" It is true that a guest does not expect to find a ring in the bathtub, but this can hardly be a working definition. Still others define quality as "giving the customer more than he or she expects." Sounds good, but if you give more than is expected today, what will be expected tomorrow? And how does one control costs with such a definition?

Although the definition "receiving more than one expects" is a bonus, most of us would be quite content if we received exactly what we expect, rather than more. When we go into a store to buy clothing, we expect a clean, comfortable environment, a wide selection of merchandise at an acceptable cost, an attentive sales person, knowledgeable and courteous service, expert alterations, no hidden cost surprises, and an efficient check out process. If we receive these things, we are happy. If any one part is missing, we are not happy. In our responses to the definition of quality, only 9% defined it as "conformance to standards," which, although not universal, is the most prevalent definition among experts on the subject, particularly in the service industries.

Quality is commonly defined as "conformance to standards."

3

QUALITY AT EVERY LEVEL

A follow-up question to the definition question asked participants if they think a Rolls Royce is a quality car. Virtually everyone thought it was. What about the Ritz Carlton hotel chain, winner of the Malcolm Baldrige National Quality Award? The consensus is that the chain is quality. Respondents also agreed that pheasant under glass would be a quality meal. But when I asked if the McDonald restaurant chain was quality, there was some debate. This raises a major point of great importance. The McDonald's chain is most probably a better example of quality that any of the 3 high-priced examples given. In terms of conforming to standards, a Big Mac in Moose Jaw, Montana, will be the same as a Big Mac in Moscow, Russia. Quality has nothing to do with price, i.e., market level. It has to do with meeting the expectations of the consumer at all market levels. Diners at McDonalds know that they are not going to have filet mignon, but they did not go there expecting it. They went knowing exactly what McDonalds offers and at what price level and they went there in anticipation of having their expectations met exactly. The odds are excellent that their expectations were met.

It is up to the business owner/manager to decide at what market level he or she wishes to operate. This is not always an easy task, requiring extensive market studies, effective analysis, and, in many cases, a bit of luck. Quality or not, many businesses do not succeed because of reasons having nothing to do with conforming to standards. The Edsel car, introduced by Ford in 1957, is a good example of a highly researched product that failed. Although somewhat innovative, the luxury model was introduced first under a cloak of marketing intrigue but, unfortunately, in a down year for auto sales, especially luxury "gas guzzlers." When the cloak of secret intrigue was lifted, the public, whose expectations for innovation were high, were disappointed, and only 66,000 of the projected 200,000 cars were sold that year. Thus, no matter how good a product might be, it can still fail through poor marketing decisions. Assuming that the marketing is correct, however, quality must be present for success, the point being that quality is crucial at every market level and does not relate specifically to price.

Quality applies to every market level from economy to luxury.

4

DEFINITION OF A STANDARD

Once people analyze and accept the definition that quality is conformance to standards, the next step is to define "standard." The definitions vary, but, in the end, when asked, people generally accept the suggestion that a standard is a "desired level of performance." Unfortunately, this definition will prevent a true program of excellence. It is easy to understand why management personnel think in terms of "desire." They have had years of experience with employees and have come to believe that error is inevitable; that employees, being human, have a certain amount of nonconformance built in. They believe that "to err is human" and nothing they say or do will ever eliminate human error. The fact is that errors are not inevitable, and although they sometimes happen, there is always a good reason, which can be addressed to prevent repetition of the error. The only acceptable definition for a standard is "a ***required*** level of performance." Standards are to be met each and every time, without fail. If such cannot happen, the standard must be changed so that 100% compliance is possible. There is a belief among some managers that motivation can be achieved by setting standards just beyond the reach of the employee so that the employee is constantly struggling to comply. This is simply not true. Failure to meet standards that are too high is a de-motivator and teaches us to accept error as an inevitable part of doing business.

Let's look at some examples. Assume you are an army paratrooper. Does it inspire confidence in you to hear that it is a desire that your parachute be packed properly? Would you not feel better knowing that it is a requirement that the parachute be safe? What about the surgeon performing your triple heart bypass? Are you comfortable hearing that it is a desire that the heart-lung machine work properly? Would you be more comfortable knowing that it is a requirement? And the young mother with a two-year-old child. Does she desire that the child stay out of the street, or is that a requirement?

It has been said that work is basically a gift that employees give to their organization. When that gift is given perfectly each and every time, the worker develops pride; especially if he or she is personally recognized for the quality of the work. It is pride that enhances performance even more.

Unless the reader now accepts the premise that standards must be required levels of performance, the excellence structure will be weak because it is built on an unsafe foundation.

Standards are required levels of performance.

5

CHARACTERISTICS OF A STANDARD

The writing of a standard would appear at first glance to be a rather easy task, but this is far from true. Two problems make writing standards difficult. First is the process of communications made difficult by the fact that, traditionally, in the hospitality industry, there are substantial cultural, economic and educational differences between the production level and the management level. I am not speaking of understanding and applying the necessary skills to perform assigned tasks. I am referring only to the process of communication. Management often tends to speak in terms understandable to management but not to the audience they are trying to influence. In such a situation communications becomes difficult and many times ineffective. Let me illustrate by an example personally encountered by me while serving as Vice President of Harvard University. Following a meeting of Deans I confessed to the President of the University that I often failed to understand what the Deans were trying to communicate. The President confessed that he, too, sometimes was lost to the conversation. "The Deans," he explained, "sometimes unknowingly lapse into "academic jargon" a use of words they easily understood but not so easily understood by those outside their circle." It was an unintentional act on their part, often not realizing they were doing it. Management level persons in hospitality sometimes have the same difficulties communicating with their employees. They speak in terms understood by management but not effectively understood by those they are trying to influence. This is why standards are best written by, and in conjunction with, those who will be complying with them.

Second, there is a tendency for managers to write too many standards, especially at the onset of a program. Think of this second point in terms of a football coach who has a playbook of 200 plays and variations. The successful coach starts off with a few basic plays and gradually adds more as the concepts are understood by the players. Many managers tend to require that someone complete the operations manual before the program is started. Given that 100% compliance is our goal, it is important that employee confidence be built slowly and steadily by implementing a few standards and then steadily adding more. This, of course, speaks to a new program for excellence. In the situation where the book of standards has already been developed, the concept of implementation involves training employees slowly and steadily and not throwing the whole book at them at one time. The concept is somewhat akin to an ocean wave, in that success begins slowly and then builds to a powerful force.

To be effective, standards must be attainable, clear, concise, in writing, and measurable. Avoid the temptation of writing standards that are too difficult to attain. For example, a standard that states that employees should be available for duty within 15 minutes of punching in on the time clock sounds like a good standard but is only so if the linen room is efficient in issuing uniforms, if there are not too many messages on the information board, and if the elevators are reasonably available. If employees are late in meeting the standard and are constantly criticized, they will be de-motivated because compliance is out of their control. The same would hold true regarding long lines at check-in or checkout if there is insufficient staff. To have standards that cannot be attained consistently is to render the standard invalid and simply trains employees that standards are not taken seriously.

That all relevant employees must understand the standard goes without saying. Proper communications are crucial to any well-run organization, and ambiguous standards are not helpful. A while back, some hotel chains took great pride in their standard that employees could make decisions to award compensation to guests encountering problems. For example, the bellman could offer an amenity if there was a problem checking in such as the room not being ready. And the waitress could give an amenity if a meal came out not prepared as ordered. These practices have generally disappeared because the guideline could not be precise and because it gave too much latitude to the employee. The idea had some merit but should have been delegated to the front desk supervisor and the dining room supervisor, who were properly trained in applying the standard. Rather than concentrating on placating the guest when an error occurs, it is better to concentrate on eliminating the error in the first place

A standard that is not in writing is a weak standard. First, putting the standard in writing means it is properly communicated and that knowledge of it cannot be questioned. Second, written standards show commitment, which is essential. Third, writing the standards assures that they are not performed intermittently. For example, airline pilots prepare for a trip by going over a readiness checklist item by item, something they have done a thousand times before. They do not rely on their memory, which, under stress, can fail them. Written standards, reviewed periodically, ensure that the checklists are valid and in use.

Standards must be measurable. It is said that you cannot manage anything you cannot measure. A standard that says that check-in lines will be no greater than 4 guests long before a swing clerk moves in to assist means that the assistant manager and/or front office manager must check the line during busy time to assure compliance. If there is no checking, the standard soon becomes irrelevant. Some standards are more difficult to check. If a standard calls for the bell person to inform the guest of hotel services enroute to the room, it is hard to observe the process. However, random calls to the guest to inquire if everything is in order and if the services have been communicated will solve the problem. And a standard that no guest will be taken to a room that is not properly made up and ready is difficult to check because it is not the kind of thing that is readily admitted, but the bell person has a good handle on the situation because he or she was in the position of defending the property and solving the problem when it occurred.

It is crucial in the process of quality assurance that the standards be taken seriously and be done correctly with the user in mind at all times.

Standards are attainable, clear, concise, in writing, and measurable levels of required performance.

ERRORS

6

THE COST OF ERROR

When a standard has not been met completely, it is an error, and errors are very costly for the hospitality industry. The industry has heretofore not developed a good method of determining the cost of an error primarily because there is so much probability involved; however, the logical use of probability is exactly what makes such a calculation possible. Most managers have no clue as to how much errors cost their operation. The consensus estimate from surveys is 3%, but studies indicate that the figure is more like 20–30%. Imagine what your bottom line would look like if you could reduce costs by 20%. Not only that, imagine the increase in sales you would enjoy if you eliminated error in your operation. Before we look at a sample calculation, it should be pointed out that the true value of a cost of error calculation is not just to develop the cost but, rather, to create an awareness of the magnitude of the cost of error.

Assume that we have a 300-room hotel averaging 75% occupancy with an average rate of $150 per night and an average stay of 1.8 nights. Further, assume that a bell person is paid $8 per hour, a Front Office Clerk is paid $12 per hour, an Assistant Manager is paid $20 per hour, and an amenity costs $10.

Now, let's examine the cost of taking a guest to a room that is not ready for occupancy.
The first step is to analyze all of the possible consequences of this error.

- The guest will not stay at your hotel on his/her next trip to that city.
- The bell person loses 15 minutes placating the guest. (It is interesting to note at this point that the bell person is now the key figure in regaining the guest's composure and understanding. This is not the role of the bell person. At this point, he or she is doing management's work.)
- The Front Desk Clerk loses 5 minutes reassigning the room.
- An amenity is given to the guest.
- An Assistant Manager calls to apologize and loses 5 minutes of time.

Next, we calculate the cost of each consequence.

ID	CONSEQUENCE	COST
1	Guest won't return (1.8 x $150 x 1.20)*	$324.00
2	Bell person loses 15 minutes	2.00
3	Front Desk Clerk loses 5 minutes	1.00
4	Assistant Manager loses 5 minutes	1.66
5	An amenity is given	10.00
	Total cost	$338.66

* We must add 20% to calculated room revenue to account for ancillary services such as food, valet, newsstand, laundry, telephone etc.

We know that not every consequence happens every time, so we must now estimate the percentage of times a consequence might happen and calculate the expected cost of the error. Estimating these percentages accurately makes for an interesting discussion with department heads!

ID	CONSEQUENCE	COST	PR	EXPECTED COST
1	Guest won't return	$324.00	.1	$32.40
2	Bell person loses 15 minutes	2.00	.75*	1.50
3	Front Desk Clerk loses 5 minutes	1.00	1.0	1.00
4	Assistant Manager loses 5 minutes	1.66	.5**	.83
5	An amenity is given	10.00	.20	2.00
	Expected cost			**$37.73**

* Not every guest is roomed by a bell person.

** Not all Assistant Managers call, although perhaps they should!

If our assumptions are close to correct, it means that every time a guest is taken to a room that is not ready, it could cost the hotel $37.73. The question now is, "How many times per year could the error happen and how many times a year does it happen?"

There are 45,625 check-ins per year ((.75 occupancy rate x 300 rooms x 365 days) divided by 1.8 average stay = 45,625).

To answer the question "How many times per year do we check guests into rooms that are not ready", the best sources are the bell staff and the front desk clerks. Let us assume that it only happens once out of every 200 check-ins, so it will happen 228 times per year (45,625 divided by 200).

If our estimates are close to accurate, the annual cost of taking a guest to a room that is not ready is $8,602 per year. If total sales are $14,782,500 , this one error represents .00058 of sales, which is a rather small consequence; however, this is only one error. It must be pointed out that we have not taken into account the negative word of mouth that errors cause. Nor have we taken into account the negative effect on staff caused by errors. A staff member exposed to what he or she considers management inefficiency is a staff member prone to make additional errors.

What about other common errors: a guest who has been walked (confirmed reservation dishonored), a meal that is not as ordered, room service that is late or forgotten, VIP mail that is not delivered, a car that is damaged in valet parking, a bad credit card that was not checked, and so on? When you consider all of the individual errors that can and do occur, the total cost will be considerably higher than 3% of sales. But what if the managers are correct and the total cost of error is only 3% of sales? In our example, that would represent a cost of $443,475 ($14,782,500 sales x .03 estimated cost of error). I would argue that $443,475 is well worth worrying about, especially if the cost to recover it is much less. But what if our 20% estimate is correct? The annual cost would be $2,956,500! ($14,782,500 sales x .20 estimated cost of error). It is safe to say that the truth lies somewhere between $443,475 and $2,956,500. Managers find this hard to believe but we have done the calculations many times with the same results. Errors cost!

In conclusion, an error is not a good event under any circumstances and should be eliminated.

An error is a standard not met, and every error is costly.

7

A LOOK AT SIX SIGMA

We have all watched in awe as a space vehicle leaves the launch pad. However, I doubt that many of us have stopped to consider all the events and processes that have to be 100% correct for the launch to succeed. There is zero tolerance for error.

A new program has evolved in the discipline of quality that emphasizes the quest for perfection in dramatic terms. It is known as Six Sigma and establishes levels of error with related cost implications. Although it focuses primarily on manufacturing operations, it does relate philosophically with the Journey to Excellence program contained herein. As stated, Six Sigma is dramatic.

For example, a Six Sigma quality level would permit no more than 3.4 errors in 1 million opportunities. For a typist, for example, this would mean no more than 1 typing error per 3,289 keystrokes, or roughly 1 typing error per 168 pages of typing. The goal is laudable, the attainment difficult. Whereas typing skills represent an interaction between a skilled person and a machine, this does not easily translate to interactions between 2 persons such as an employee and a guest. To seek to have no more than one error in interactions between a front desk clerk and a guest assumes that all guests are alike and arrive at the desk with totally similar psychological baggage and likewise for the clerk. But Guest A arrives already running late for a meeting, Guest B arrives just after receiving a disturbing call from home, Guest C arrives not feeling well, and so on. In similar fashion, the clerk arrives after hearing that a guest was just taken to a room not yet ready for occupancy, or just after the computers suffered a 15-minute downtime, and so forth. Basically, many hospitality interactions are between 2 individuals with constantly changing situations. This adds a great handicap burden on error-free transactions. It does not mean a Six Sigma goal is invalid for hospitality. It just means that attaining Six Sigma is exponentially more difficult to attain. However, accepting less than 100% error-free transactions is to guarantee that errors will occur, whereas seeking 100% achievement may still result in errors, but fewer and fewer over time.

Although a Six Sigma performance may not be practical for Hospitality, the goal of zero errors remains relevant.

8

THE BLACK SWAN EVENT

As we conclude our discussion of the cost of error, it is important to understand the black swan event first introduced by Nassim Nicholas Taleb in his 2007 book *The Black Swan*. The genesis is that, for years, it was believed that swans were always white in color, until black swans were discovered in Australia. This discovery, of course, caused a complete change in perception, leading Taleb to define a black swan event as an event that:

- is a surprise;
- has a major impact; and
- after it occurs, is rationalized by hindsight.

In short, black-swan events are unplanned, are unexpected, and have serious consequences, such as the following examples:

Legionnaires ' disease: "The Bellevue-Stratford Hotel, in Philadelphia, Pennsylvania, gained worldwide notoriety in July 1976, when it hosted a statewide convention of the American Legion. Soon after, a pneumonia-like disease killed thirty-four people and sickened 221 more who had been in the hotel. The vast majority were members of the convention. The negative publicity caused the hotel to close in November 1976. In 1977, Dr. Joseph McDade discovered a new bacterium, which was identified as the causative organism. The bacterium was named *Legionella* and the disease, legionellosis, after the first victims. It was found to live, among other places, in the cooling water of air-conditioning systems, like that atop the Bellevue-Stratford, which had spread it throughout the hotel." (From Wikipedia, the free encyclopedia)

Hotel Sabre System Failure: In his book ***Software Failure: Management Failure—Amazing Stories and Cautionary Tales***, Stephen Flowers analyzes legendary IT failures. Again and again, the failures are attributed to: information errors, inadequate testing, complexity, lack of communication, high levels of uncertainty and high stakes. The Sabre computer reservation system, such a success for American Airlines that it became more profitable than the airline itself, would become a fiasco for the Hilton Hotels, Marriott, Budget Rent-a-Car and AMR Information Services joint venture, named Confirm. The development budget for the Confirm CRS system for booking hotel rooms and rental cars was $125 million in 1988. By 1992, however, instead of making 10 times the estimated sales of $3.1m, the system was written off and the partners sued each other for an undisclosed amount, but rumored to be in the millions. They settled discreetly out of court. (From Computergram, 28 May 1997)

Hyatt Regency Hotel Walkway Collapse: The Hyatt Regency hotel walkway collapse during a tea dance was a major disaster that occurred on July 17, 1981 in Kansas City, Missouri, killing 114 people and injuring more than 200 others. At the time it was the deadliest structural collapse in U.S. history. (From Wikipedia, the free encyclopedia)

Generally speaking, we think of errors in more unspectacular terms. A guest who is served an unacceptable meal, an undelivered VIP message, and missing luggage all require some form of gratuitous response yet are not catastrophic events. They are, in fact, somewhat common events with limited exposure and minor consequences. The black swan event, by contrast, has major consequences if handled incorrectly. Unfortunately, because of their unexpected nature, black swan events are rarely pre-analyzed regarding their impact. The Tylenol Cyanide Lacing Event, discussed further on, is a prime example of proper preparation and response. Whereas most observers predicted the demise of Tylenol when the catastrophe occurred, the demise did not happen, because of President James Burke's response. Hotel chains are particularly vulnerable to black swan events because such an event in one property has such a carryover effect chain-wide.

The consequences of a black swan event make the prevention of errors a crucial concern.

JOURNEY TO EXCELLENCE

9

WHAT ABOUT EXCELLENCE?

Thus far, we have discussed quality as it has developed over the years. We have emphasized the consistent conformance to standards. And we have come to realize that all errors, whatever their magnitude, are costly and to be avoided. This brings us to our prime objective, the concept of excellence. What, then, is excellence, and how does it differ from quality?

I once gave a lecture on quality to an audience on the island of Curacao. I stayed in a well-known hotel, part of an international chain. When I checked out, there was a charge of $75 US for a 5-minute call I had made to France. When I protested, I was told that that is what the telephone company charged the hotel. But when I checked with the phone company, something a typical guest would never do, I learned that the charge to the hotel was $28 US. The mark-up was 268%. It seems that the hotel had a standard to egregiously inflate international phone calls on the basis that few guests, in their haste to check out, would not even question the charge. I vowed that I would never stay in that chain of hotels again, and I have been true to my word.

Many properties have standards regarding maintenance and maintenance costs. By viewing maintenance costs as a percent of sales rather than as necessary tasks to be performed despite cost, you are placing the safety of the guest in jeopardy. Fire alarm systems that are not checked regularly could fail when needed. Air filters that are not cleaned regularly cause air-conditioning failures. Refrigerators that are not maintained can result in health issues through improper storage temperatures. Unsafe storage of flammable materials causes fire hazards.

The infamous DuPont Plaza Hotel fire in Puerto Rico in December of 1986 is a good example of improper standards. The hotel, in the midst of a labor dispute, was warned that a fire might be set and did little to follow up. The origin of the fire was traced to furniture and trash stored improperly and illegally in a hallway. Several exit doors were locked to "control alleged employee pilferage." The general alarm was not activated because of a decision "not to alarm the guests." Elevator shafts as well as ductwork were improperly sealed, permitting the fire to spread rapidly throughout the hotel. There were no automatic fire-detection systems to alert guests. Further, in an attempt to save money, the 7-property chain had reduced liability insurance to a total chain-wide exposure of $1 million. These unfortunate events were the result of placing economic concerns above guest safety.

Ninety-six persons perished in the DuPont Plaza fire. In a frantic effort to survive, the chain sought to make the case that the DuPont Plaza was not an integral part of the chain (better to lose one property than impact the entire 7-property chain.) The jury didn't buy the argument, and the case was settled for $129 million, causing the chain to sell some of its properties.

On a more mundane, but also more prevalent, note, what about a standard that encourages overbooking to ensure high occupancy? Other than health and safety issues, a walked guest is among the most costly of errors.

The point is that compliance to standards is only meaningful if the standards are "right." The introduction of "right" introduces ethics to the equation. We are now concerned with total compliance to right standards, and when this happens, we are no longer talking quality, and we are talking excellence. ***"Excellence*** is the inseparable union of quality (consistency) and ethics (being right). Let us now discuss the meaning and implications of ethics.

Excellence is the inseparable union of
quality (consistency)
and ethics (right).

THE CASE FOR ETHICS

10

WHAT IT MEANS TO BE "ETHICAL"

The word "ethics" stems from the Greek word "ethos," which means "character." Thus, ethics, in general, is the study of character or what makes us who we are. We are interested in how we achieve a good character, that is, what it means to "be ethical." The study of being ethical is a classic example of paralysis by analysis. By and large, the study of ethics has been taken over by philosophers who become enmeshed in the search for the source of ethics and the elusive absolute ethic (i.e., the body of ethics that is universally and equally applicable to all humans). It becomes very confusing to the practicing businessperson who would like to embrace ethical principles and believes they are essential but does not know how to proceed. In every seminar in which I am involved, I ask participants if they believe in being ethical, and the answer is overwhelmingly "yes." But when I ask participants to define just what being ethical means, there is far less agreement. In November of 2005, I surveyed executives in 500 American Hotel & Lodging Association (AH&LA) hotels over 300 rooms and received 224 responses to the request to "define ethics." There were 32 different approaches to the definition in the responses. This is not too surprising when you consider that *The International Encyclopedia of Ethics* (Fitzroy Dearborn Publishers, Chicago, IL) lists some 91 theoretical approaches to ethics. Sadly, 20.5% of the respondents in our survey left the question blank. However, 23% included the word "right" in their definition while another 21% mentioned "morality." Ethics and morality are interrelated in most people's minds. If we were to try to differentiate, it could be generalized that ethics deals with "right and wrong" and morality deals with "good and evil." In the case of both ethics and morality, the source of determining what is "right" or "good" is generally attributed to that higher power referred to in most societies as God. This, in my opinion is why many people shy away from referring to ethics and embracing ethics in the development of their standards. No one has ever seen "God," nor has God ever revealed himself or herself except through the writing of humans and an occasional reference to hearing God's voice. As an ordained minister (Harvard M/Div 1988), I believe strongly in God and in God's guidance of my life through prayer. I am not alone in my belief. But that is not our issue here. We are concerned with a working definition of being ethical that can guide our business decisions, and we are not too pleased to accept others telling us how God wants us to act. If we are to embrace being ethical, we need a more pragmatic definition and objective source of what is "right."

I would propose as a definition of what it is to be ethical "knowing what is right and having the will to do it." It would be easier to define acting ethically as "doing right things," but I believe my definition is better because it establishes responsibility. If a person does not know what is "right," he or she cannot be blamed for not acting rightly. This establishes the supervisor as responsible for teaching and the employee as responsible for learning. The question of having the will to act rightly given the proper knowledge places the responsibility on the employee to act and the supervisor to ensure that the action is correct. Responsibility is key to acting ethically both on an organizational level and on a personal level. This is what makes the hospitality industry so unique. If we are manufacturing a car, the objective is for every assembly function to be done correctly. For the most part, we are dealing with a repetitive process involving an inanimate object— the employee Bob attaches the steering wheel to car after car all day long. And Bob never meets the customer who buys the car. In the hospitality industry, there is far more interaction with the customer and the interactions are seldom exactly alike. The hotel employee must accept the responsibility to represent the organization exactly as the standards have communicated it to be. And to exacerbate the issue, Bob probably has a good wage and benefit package, whereas the hospitality industry is known for low wages and minimal benefits.

If we can agree that acting ethically is defined as "knowing what is right and having the will to do it," we are ready to move on to the basic question "How do we know what is right?"

Being ethical is "knowing what is right and having the will to do it."

11

THE NEED FOR A SIMPLIFIED BASE FOR ETHICS

We have discussed the difficulty in accepting ethics when it is based on an absolute perceived word from a higher power interpreted through humans who claim to understand that power. Although schools of Hotel, Restaurant and Institutional Management (HRI) profess an interest in ethics, according to my survey of more than 300 schools of HRI in the world, fewer than 10% have any sort of course addressing the subject, and even that 10% is suspect. (Incidentally, of the responses to my 500 hotel survey previously noted, 71% participants believe that schools of HRI are not doing a good job teaching ethics, 7% think they are, and 22% don't know.) This makes sense, as virtually no schools of HRI teach ethics. I asked respondents, all General Managers or Department Heads, if they would like to know more about ethics. Of the respondents who ventured an opinion, 260 (69%) said "yes", 24% said "no" and 7% said they "didn't know." Interestingly, in his book ***"Our Underachieving Colleges"*** (2007, Princeton University Press)," author Derek Bok, past President of Harvard University, stated "According to a recent survey of more than 112,000 undergraduates, two thirds of all Freshmen consider it "essential" and "very important" that colleges help them develop their personal values." You can hypothesize from the Bok survey that schools of HRI are also not meeting the personal needs of students in the area of ethics.

In another question in my survey, I asked respondents if they had a published, visible code of ethics. Eighty-six properties responded. Of the 86, 29 were single responses (only one respondent from that property). These 29 single responses said yes. Another 23 properties had multiple responses all saying "yes." This means that there is complete agreement, according to the responses from 52 properties that said they had a published code. From another 21 properties with multiple responses, we had disagreement as to whether a published code existed. It would seem that a visible code should be pretty obvious. At any rate, I then sent a letter to those 52 properties that agreed they had a published code and the 21 who disagreed. I asked them to share their code with us. Because their code is allegedly published, there should have been no problem. I received 6 codes! It would seem that respondents had concluded that it would be perceived as good if they had a published code, whether or not it was true. While responses to surveys are traditionally not good in numbers, I have found that when hoteliers have positive things to say, the response is generally quite good. I assumed that there would be a certain pride in having a published code and that the response from 73 properties who claimed to have a code would exceed 6 respondents.

It is premature to draw a general conclusion from the data. Further study is required, but I would share the personal perception that hoteliers believe that ethics is important; they don't feel that they are receiving help in the area, and they would like to know more about ethics. I believe that this perception is strongly supported by yet another question on the survey: "Do you think the Hospitality Industry should focus on ethics?" Ninety eight percent said "yes," and 2% said "no." Why, then, if hoteliers want more knowledge, if they want schools of HRI to teach ethics, if they believe ethics is important, and if they want their industry to become more involved in ethics, is ethics not being addressed at any level? I believe that the subject of ethics has been made too complicated by a philosophical mindset that tends to address questions where there are no answers rather than apply ethics in a practical, usable way. We need a simple, basic understanding of ethics.

The subject of ethics is important to hoteliers but is made difficult in application by becoming too complicated by philosophy.

Complicating ethics by becoming too philosophical is limiting its acceptance and use

12

INTRODUCING A SIMPLIFIED BASIS FOR ETHICS

To begin our discussion of a new and simplified basis for ethics, we need to ask the question "Are we guaranteed any rights at birth?" It has been said that the only true right we have at birth is the right to control that property which is legally ours. "Property" has several faces. Our bodies are our fundamental property. Anyone who impacts our body in a negative way is infringing upon our natural right. If we can agree that it would be unethical to injure in any way the body of another person, then, of course, murder and physical abuse would obviously be unethical. So would false imprisonment and slavery. It would be unethical for a doctor to be guilty of malpractice. Child abuse would also be unethical.

Another property given to us by virtue of birth would be our image, that is, our reputation. Thus, false witness and slander would be unethical. We also count as our property all the material things that we have legally acquired: home, furnishings, car, clothes, etc. Stealing would be unethical, as would any kind of damage we might inflict on the material property of others. We also have intellectual property; the thoughts and ideas that we originate and own. Thus plagarism is unethical.

A property that is a bit more difficult to define is what I will call space. As individuals, we are entitled to certain peace of mind. The founding fathers recognized this when they wrote in the Declaration of Independence that we are given the unalienable rights of life, liberty and the pursuit of happiness. It is interesting to note that Thomas Jefferson's original draft of the Declaration spoke of life, liberty and property. However, subsequent debate changed property to pursuit of happiness in order not to become entangled with the questionable English notions of ownership of property. As an example of space, consider the situation where a worker is harassed to vote a certain way in an election under the implied threat of physical harm. Whether or not the harm is real, the threat of it causes a negative impact of peace of mind, pursuit of happiness, if you will, and is thus considered unethical. On a larger scale, consider how the Israelis must feel believing as they do that Iran is working to develop nuclear weapons which ultimately could be used against them. All the Iranian denials in the world cannot give Israel peace of mind. Although no physical change has been made to any Israeli property the threat of harm affects the Israeli space and is unethical.

A word about the role of conscience as a determinant of ethics. I do not believe that we are born with a "right" conscience in place, although many do believe that our conscience comes at birth from a higher power that is pure. I believe that our environment shapes our conscience as we develop. For example, if you were born in the Deep South prior to the Civil War, it might not bother your conscience to see blacks denied the right to vote and forced to attend segregated schools (if they were schooled at all). Obviously, if you thought about this in terms of denying blacks that property that was theirs, you would take a different view; however, the denial of these rights to blacks in that era was a result of unethical laws. It was, in many parts of the South, lawful to deny basic rights to blacks. For example, when Rosa Parks, on December 1, 1955, refused to ride in the back of the bus, she was breaking the law. But the law was an unethical law and was subsequently changed.

The question of law will be discussed in more detail later on. For now, let's take another look at conscience. Many people believe that punishing children physically is unethical. Others believe that controlled physical punishment, a spanking, for example, is acceptable to make a point of correction. Is either point of view wrong other than in the minds of the individuals? What about keeping animals in cages in a zoo? Animal rights activists are against the idea, while most others are not. Both sides are acting in good conscience, their individual good conscience. In such instances of conflicting conscience, special mediation is required. Usually, this takes the input of the legal system to define the issue and set the boundaries. In other issues, there are conflicting points of view that are not clarified by law. Many people believe that it was unethical to drop the atom bomb on Hiroshima and Nagasaki during WWII. No amount of debate will resolve this issue. It is a matter of personal belief. The fact that different cultures as well as elements within a single culture have different interpretations of "right" is, to me, the best argument against a single source of an absolute, all encompassing conscience. Thus, while conscience is definitely a person's property, it is not something the person is born with and therefore is not an absolute basis for ethical judgment.

Rather than getting all caught up in the deeply profound, and confusing, issues of ethical thought, I propose that we simply define the body of ethics as respecting the lawful property of others.

Ethics is based on the right of a person or entity to control property that is legally owned.

13

ANOTHER ASPECT OF ETHICS

The astute reader will challenge our definition of ethics at this point by arguing that it does not go far enough. The property does not cover many areas that are deemed ethical but have no negative impact on property. For example, it could be argued that an ethical person would stop to aid an elderly person who had fallen. An ethical person would contribute cash to help a poor family put food on the table, and an ethical person would help tutor a child having difficulty in school. In each of these cases, the individuals are not preventing a negative impact on another person's property. They are, in fact, adding value. Property is still involved. In the first two cases, it is physical property. In the third case, it is intellectual property. It would be a hard sell to call someone unethical for not stopping to help an injured person, not contributing to the needy, or not performing tutoring services. But it is very easy to call those who do such things ethical in their actions.

We need to keep in mind that ethics refers to one's character, and that varies from individual to individual and is not irrevocably tied to religion. Philosophers tend to view ethics as some sort of absolute code that should be relevant to every person in the same way. In the final analysis, this comes down to humans interpreting a higher power and, as already stated, this is not acceptable to many thoughtful people. Thus, there is a sense of relativity. A person's character is judged by the situation and his or her individual deeds, not against an absolute standard. The task is to define the elements in the specific situation before deciding whether or not a particular deed is ethical or unethical. The effect that an act has upon the property of others is, for me, the only solid and logical basis for determining ethics and it may be viewed as either preventing injury to property or increasing the value of same.

Increasing the value of the property of others is also an ethical act

14

SEVEN TESTS FOR ETHICAL DECISIONS

No one is totally ethical. It can even be said that requiring someone to be totally ethical is, in fact, unethical. The reason is that there are too many variables. We are constantly faced with ethical decisions. Using the property approach can determine whether or not we have an ethical issue but it cannot determine if a particular act is, or is not, an ethical act. For example, it could be argued that insider trading is an ethical act because it improves our property; our financial resources. However, in doing so, we are not so much negatively impacting the property of others as we are denying them an opportunity to add to their own resources. And, what about "escorts" discretely working the hotel cocktail lounge? In a transaction between consenting adults, whose property is being impacted? Yet, many of us consider such activities unethical. What about a situation wherein a manager of 100 employees must terminate 10 employees to save the jobs of 90? This is a case of severely impacting the property of some to preserve the property of others. What does acting ethically mean in this case? We need a process to guide us through such dilemmas.

I have found a process called "seven tests for acting ethically" to be most helpful. The seven tests are in the form of questions that should become ingrained in all individuals and used almost unconsciously to help decide questions of ethics:

- Is what I am deciding legal?
- Will my decision hurt anyone?
- Is my decision fair?
- Am I being honest?
- Can I live with my decision?
- Would I be willing to publicly announce my decision?
- What if everyone did what I am about to do?

Each of these seven tests will be discussed in order; however, I would like to begin by making a general comment. Although each test is valid, it is not final in its own right. Take the case of Rosa Parks in Montgomery, discussed previously. Although we would all consider it unethical to force her to ride in the back of the bus, that was the law of the time; thus, the legal test would not decide the issue. The fairness test is more appropriate. The seven tests must be viewed and used in total. While a particular issue may pass several of the tests, it is pretty much assured that if it fails one or more of them, it is a questionable ethical decision and must be carefully evaluated. By the same token, if the decision in question can pass all of the tests, you are pretty much assured of having made the most ethical decision. But the answers to some of the questions can be in debate, as in the atom-bomb example. Whether or not use of the atom bomb was fair still remains debatable more than six decades after the fact. In short, the seven test process, while not an unimpeachable test, nevertheless, when applied with thought, can assure with high probability that a decision is ethical. If we carefully analyze all of our decisions with the seven test questions, we will undoubtedly be considered a highly ethical person but we still may, albeit rarely, make an unethical decision. Factors that reinforce this statement are discussed below

TIME	The decision might need to be made before all the facts and options are known. A law enforcement officer who harms a suspect whom he truly believes has a weapon and is about to use it is acting ethically whether or not it is subsequently shown that no weapon existed. Time did not permit more than a split second to make the decision.
FACTS	Sometimes all the facts are not known when the decision is made. The Iraq War was considered by most to be an ethical decision based on weapons of mass destruction, which proved later to be problematic.
ENVIRONMENT	Sometimes our upbringing clouds our ability to definitively know what is right. Being raised in a household of racial prejudice often results in unethical decisions until truth ultimately prevails.
PRESSURE	There are situations when job security is in danger unless the requests from superiors to lie are obeyed. Although this in no way excuses unethical behavior, it does tend to explain it.

Before we begin discussing the seven tests in order, let us pose an ethical dilemma that can be evaluated by each test. This scenario is common to virtually every hotel in the world that has a cocktail lounge.

A very attractive and well-groomed thirty-something "lady of the night" (let us call her Vanessa") is "working the room." She is seated at the bar, having a cocktail and greeting the occasional male patron who approaches her with a smile, often having a drink with him. She is very well behaved. The bartender has noticed that on several occasions when men look into the room, they often enter when they become aware of this lady's presence. She seems to be good for business. The bartender has also noticed that she leaves alone from time to time for approximately an hour but always returns except when closing hour is approaching. She frequents the hotel three and sometimes four times a week. The hotel staff knows and likes her even though they are aware that she is there on business. This has been going on for almost two years now, and there has never been a problem involving her.

This scenario has been posed to managers and department heads in surveys around the world. The question is "Is this an ethical issue or not?" The response is close to the same in every instance: 70% of the respondents do not believe this is an ethical issue. They believe that it is not up to the hotel to legislate the morality of individuals. What would our seven tests say about the situation?

Acting ethically, a journey rather than a destination, requires that every decision be carefully evaluated from many perspectives.

15

IS MY DECISION LEGAL?

The laws of all civilized nations and even those we might not consider to be civilized are based on "protecting what is right." Most nations have a system of peers who judge right from wrong after hearing all the facts involved. There are methods to deal with laws that were duly enacted and subsequently brought into question by factors that developed. As a general statement, if a decision is totally acceptable under existing law, it is presumed to be "right" and therefore ethical. It is very proper that the first test should be asking whether the decision is legal, yet we have already seen in the case of Rosa Parks that being legal does not always mean being ethical. In her case, no consideration was taken of the damage to her self-image; her "property," that resulted from the demeaning act of forcing her, albeit legally, to sit in a segregated section of the bus. The same could be said of the struggle for women to gain the right to vote. For 140-plus years, until the 19th amendment to the constitution was passed in 1920, it was illegal for American women to vote. The statement that "all men (people) were created equal" had little meaning for the law banning equality to women. Another very strong issue with the law and the question of ethics has to do with abortion. Many believe that the fetus is the property of the mother until birth and that the mother can therefore opt to abort her fetus. Others believe that the fetus has life at the point of conception and aborting the fetus is therefore to put to death a living being (destroying that being's property). The law makes abortions legal but does not resolve the ethical issue that is brought into question over the debate as to when life begins for the fetus. The point is that testing a decision as being ethical or not by asking if it is legal works in the majority of cases but not all. It is a good first question but is not absolute.

What about our working girl in the bar? Are Vanessa's activities legal? No, the laws are very clear about public solicitation for prostitution; however, our working girl is not soliciting, at least not overtly. If there is overt solicitation going on, it is the men soliciting her; thus, although everyone knows what is happening; no one is willing to raise the question of law. If money exchanges hands in the guest's room, it is a different situation, clearly a case of prostitution, but there are no witnesses and thus no case unless brought by the male partner, who is unlikely to do so unless some form of deceit has taken place. I would argue that our "working girl" example, as described, is clearly illegal but done in such a manner as to make the law unenforceable. You can say that the test of law in this case is not a persuasive argument to rate the situation as unethical.

"Is my decision legal?" is an excellent first test but not absolute in helping us decide what is ethical.

16

WILL MY DECISION HURT ANYONE?

It is unavoidable that decisions in business and personal life can cause others to be hurt. Wedding invitations that exclude children frequently cause family disputes. Executors charged with distributing assets will often cause hurt when heirs' expectations are not met. Calling an executive in from vacation to help at a crisis time will cause frustration and hurt. Reducing dividends causes hurt for those who depend on the income. And, of course, when a company needs to downsize, those terminated are hurt. These, however, are business decisions, not ethical decisions. To believe that a business decision means that no one is ever hurt is totally unreasonable. At the same time, it is unethical to inflict hurt on others. The ethical approach is not to eliminate hurt when it is impossible to do so; rather, it is to be aware of the hurt inflicted and take all possible steps to minimize it.

Business is bad, and survival means recouping the wages and benefits of 10 out of 100 of your employees. Certainly, it would be advantageous to terminate 10 employees who are close to vesting their retirement benefits. And we could use this opportunity to terminate Charley, who, as the employee representative, often is a nuisance to management. Or we can decide who goes on the basis of how much they make—highest wages go first. Although these solutions might be in the best financial interest of the company, the negative effect on the company image will undoubtedly cause problems further on. Inflicting insensitive hurt on others is both unethical and counterproductive.

However, we can work to minimize the hurt by offering an optional early retirement plan. Or we could keep all employees and everyone could agree to a temporary reduction in pay. Further, we could explore whether some employees would actually appreciate temporary unpaid leaves of absence. At the least, we should look first at those with the least seniority and should offer counseling to those whom we ultimately decide to terminate.

What about Vanessa who is working the cocktail lounge? Is anyone being hurt by her behavior? If the wives of her male "friends" were to know what was taking place, there would be big hurt. And if she transmitted an STD such as AIDS, it would be a major hurt. Or if she were disposed toward theft of her partner's wallet, for example, this could hurt. And, of course, if the hotel suffers a bad image as a result of her activities, that could hurt. But none of these issues are contained in the scenario as written. It could be concluded that, although the potential for hurt exists, none is taking place, and thus, our test is not productive. It would be difficult to designate the situation as unethical on the basis of hurt alone.

Often, decisions unavoidably hurt others, but an ethical decision maker will do everything possible to minimize the hurt.

17

IS MY DECISION FAIR?

Our meaning of "fair" in this test of ethical thought is "impartial," "evenhanded," and "nondiscriminatory." Many examples of unfairness, such as discrimination, are also covered under legality and hurtfulness, but not all. Let's look at an example.

Mr. and Mrs. Brown booked a weekend room two months in advance for Friday and Saturday nights at the going rate of $150 per night. Two weeks later, realizing that the particular weekend in question was going to be very slow, the management decided to offer all rooms for 30% off, or $105 per night, and feature a luau around the pool on Saturday night as incentive. The luau was offered at $30 per person, a very good price considering the setting, the menu, and the entertainment. The promotion was a success, and the hotel had reservations for all of its 250 rooms. When the weekend came, the Browns, who had been out of the country and unaware of the special promotion, arrived for their weekend stay. Should the hotel charge them $150 per night as originally agreed or offer them the new rate of $105 enjoyed by the vast majority of the other reservations that weekend?

When this scenario was presented to managers at seminars, almost 75% said they would charge $150 because "that was the agreed upon price, and a deal is a deal." It is agreed that the hotel is perfectly within its rights to continue to charge the full rate, but does it make ethical sense in terms of fairness? The line is a thin one. Management is not actually being unfair, but if fairness were brought into serious question, management might opt to give the lower rate. The only reason the Browns are on the full rate is that they were unaware of the promotion. Had they been aware, they would simply have called and asked for the promotional rate, and it undoubtedly would have been offered. Further, the Browns are customers, and the goal of all hotels is to make them repeat customers. If the Browns learn of the special promotion while also being charged the higher rate, it is highly questionable that they would participate in the luau or stay at the hotel on their next visit to that city. They might also affect others by their negative word of mouth concerning their experience. If they are freely advised and given the promotional rate, however, there is a totally positive effect. Trust in the hotel to do what is right and fair will result in repeat business and positive word of mouth from the Browns. Is it worth preserving $90 in room revenue (two nights at the reduced rate) against a probable loss of $60 plus in food and beverage revenue and potential loss of trust to insist on the original rate? Another way to view the fairness test would be to ask how you would react if you were the Browns and the hotel voluntarily gave you the promotional rate.

There are other examples of fairness in hospitality. What about the situation in which the Maître'd seats friends and VIPs and/or known high tippers ahead of those with valid reservations? What about adding a mandatory 15% service charge on food bills and giving only part of it to the server?

A major issue in most hotels is that of overbooking. After calculating a certain percent of "no shows," the hotel will overbook to compensate. Often, the no shows fail to happen in the numbers predicted, and the hotel finds itself having to book the confirmed reservation guest elsewhere, often paying transportation to take the guests to their new location and also offering some sort of amenity by way of apology. Other than cases of lawsuits, walked guests cause one of the most expensive errors possible. The chance of the guest ever returning is slight, and the negative word-of-mouth image is quite detrimental. In defense of the hotel, guests who book confirmed reservations and then do not show are themselves unethical in that they impact the profitability of the property. Today, most hotels take the valid credit card and key it to a cancellation policy that will permit them to collect whether or not the guest shows. Still, if the room can be sold twice—to the new guest and on the credit card of a no show, so much the better for the hotel. But it is decidedly unfair and unethical.

What about our working-girl scenario? Is what we are doing by permitting her activities really fair? To whom is her situation unfair? She is a paying customer for the hotel bar. There is nothing unfair about that. Her client is receiving exactly what he has purchased, so he is not being treated unfairly. And our working girl is being fairly compensated. Fairness does not seem to be an issue in our example.

Fairness, although often a thin line, is, nevertheless, a valid test for ethical decisions.

18

AM I BEING HONEST WITH MY DECISION?

It is important that ethical decisions be based on honesty. From early childhood, we have been told that we should never lie. Everyone remembers the story of George Washington, who freely admitted to his father that he cut down the cherry tree. Of course we now know that the cherry tree story itself was not true. It was an allegory about honesty. The fact is that it is never good to lie, but sometimes it is better to lie than tell the truth. And, in a strange twist, there are times when it is illegal to tell the truth. As a simple example of discretely not telling the truth, consider what you would say if the wife of the boss, wearing a hideous looking hat, asked you what you thought of it? I assume you would not tell her it was an awful choice of hats. I think you would be best advised to say something like, "It certainly is unusual." We can argue the validity of not telling the truth by acknowledging that doing so would hurt someone and that we don't want to do that. What about the terminally ill child who asks the doctor if she is going to die? The doctor now must decide if the child can handle the truth, and if the doctor decides the child cannot, he or she will withhold the truth.

Assume you are the treasurer of a major hotel chain that has been in negotiations to acquire another chain but are not yet ready to announce it. Your stockbroker neighbor confronts you and tells you he has heard rumors of the acquisition. In this example, you had better not tell the truth, or you will risk charges of insider trading and possible jail time. In another example, assume you are in union negations. You and the hotel management are willing to go a bit higher in benefits, but when the union seems ready to settle, when an employee, who is active in the union, asks you if you think management could go higher. It would be prudent not to tell the truth.

There is another role for honesty. Are we being honest in describing what we are doing, or are we rationalizing? I once worked in New York City for a senior executive of a major hotel chain. This executive was absolutely adamant regarding ethics, particularly in the area of kickbacks. My job was dealing with contractors, many of whom had contracts worth hundreds of thousands of dollars with our company. My boss made it abundantly clear that we were never to take any money or gifts from any contractor. If we had lunch or dinner, we paid. If we went to a Broadway show, we bought the tickets. The penalty for doing otherwise was that we would be terminated. Yet the executive would frequently come to New York to go to the championship heavyweight boxing matches with the contractors. He would pay for his own ticket but, invariably, to make it interesting, he and the contractors would wager on the fights, usually \$1000. The bets took the form of the contractor betting that the fight would not go beyond the first round. For anyone who follows boxing, it is extremely rare that a heavyweight bout ends so quickly; thus, my boss would invariably win the bet and collect \$1000. His rationalization was that it was a friendly bet between two parties in which he could win or lose. Because the odds were totally skewed in his favor, however, what was happening, in effect, was that my boss was being given a $1000 kickback, which, in his mind, he could defend as being ethical. Were he honest with himself, it would not have happened.

In the case of our continuing analysis of Vanessa, who has set up shop in our cocktail lounge, is there a case of dishonesty? The hotel and relevant staff know exactly what is going on. Vanessa's client knows what is happening. If the police should enter and ask Vanessa what she is doing there, she will tell the truth—she is having a drink. Lying does not seem to be part of Vanessa's scenario.

It is never right to be dishonest,
but there are times when it may be
more ethical to withhold the truth than to speak it.

19

CAN I LIVE WITH MY DECISION?

The question "Can I live with my decision" is recognizing the presence of a conscience. All persons have a sense of right and wrong, but not all persons look at situations in the same way. What is "right" for one person may be totally "wrong" for another. For example, the attacks on Pearl Harbor and the World Trade Center are considered by most Americans as totally unethical. The Japanese who attacked Pearl Harbor in 1941 and the terrorists who destroyed the World Trade Center's twin towers in 2001 did not view their acts as unethical. This raises a crucial point in the use of conscience as a test for ethics. Many persons believe that our conscience is somehow calibrated to right and wrong when we are conceived. They believe that some higher power, God, gives us a sense of what is right or wrong and that we are born with this sense. This cannot be true. If it were, there would be universality in ethical decisions. But there is not. Our consciences are formed by what we are taught both by others and by our experiences as we grow and develop. This is why slavery was considered right and proper for thousands of years and is now widely believed to be wrong. It is also why it took American women more than 300 years to gain the right to vote and why, today, large segments of the Middle East still deny that right to their women citizens. This is why legal age premarital cohabitation is accepted by much of the world but believed to be reason enough to condemn women to a death by stoning in other parts of the world. It is why we have basic disagreements about mandatory death sentences, abortions, homosexual and lesbian relationships, and conscientious objectors. Although our consciences are valuable in helping us decide ethical issues that affect us, they are not valuable in deciding the ethical decisions of others. The best we can say in such situations is that we believe what the others are doing is unethical but that it may not be unethical to them because ethics is a function of what we believe and what they believe is based on different learning experiences from ours. Most radical Muslims in the Middle East, for example, believe it is their duty to destroy those who do not accept Islam. Their authority comes from Mohammed, whose authority comes from their God Allah -while first world nations generally believe in freedom of religion and attribute it to their perception of God. During the American Civil War, both the North and the South attributed their cause as acceptable and desired by God. Etched in my mind is a large mound of graves in Monte Casino, Italy, site of a great WWII battle. The mound is terraced with graves, Allies on one side and Axis on the other. At the top are two gigantic crosses, back to back, one white on the Allied side and one black on the Axis side. Altogether, some 70,000 military lives were lost at Monte Casino, all of them while "doing God's work." I am certain that both sides truly believed that what they were doing was ethical in God's eyes.

This discussion is not meant to say that the conscience is not a valuable tool for judging the ethicality of decisions. Rather, it is intended to say that our consciences are useful in judging personal ethics but not universal ethics.

What does conscience have to say about our entrepreneur, Vanessa, in the cocktail lounge? Prostitution is a harmful activity. At least, it can create some feelings of guilt and often weakens the marriage bond and, at most, poses serious health problems. Further, prostitution is often linked to drugs, which can present safety and security problems for hotel guests who participate. Frequently, situations start out as described in our vignette, harmless enough that no one wants to make it an issue. But often, things grow worse, and more working girls (and/or boys) are attracted to the lounge, and the situation gets out of hand. It is best to curtail solicitation activities early on so they do not become more prevalent. Surveys indicate that few managers are willing to step in and ban such activities given the description we have presented. Can management live with such a discrete activity that is taking place? Apparently, they can, and conscience does not seem to be a factor. The approach seems to be that if Vanessa's conscience doesn't bother her or the "customer", and she causes no problems, it is not up to management to legislate morality.

The conscience, which dictates whether we can live with an ethical decision, is a personal choice and is difficult to apply to the choices of others except as a personal opinion.

20

WOULD I ANNOUNCE MY DECISION PUBLICLY?

Generally speaking, when people behave in a "wrong" way, they would prefer that no one know about it. In fact, a prevalent rationalization by students who cheat in school is that it is acceptable if you are not caught. In a way, this is one criticism of John Stuart Mill's utilitarian theory of right and wrong, which says that people strive to increase pleasure and decrease pain. Accordingly, increasing pleasure by doing wrong things is assumed by some to be acceptable if no one knows about it and it therefore causes no pain. The problem is that very few wrongs go unpunished in the long run, and invariably, when the truth is known, the repercussions are very damaging. There is absolutely no expectation that people should broadcast their unethical acts, but a valid test is to consider the results if others were aware of your activities. If you are engaged in activities that are best kept to yourself, there is a strong possibility that there is something wrong in what you are doing, and you should reevaluate your activities.

This is one test that helps us in our evaluation of Vanessa and her cocktail-lounge small-business venture. Although the large majority of managers polled would not take any action to curtail Vanessa's activities, neither would they be willing to admit publicly that prostitution is present in their cocktail lounge. I suspect also that they would deny knowledge of Vanessa's activities were they to be asked. Of course, the unwillingness to publicize our activities is not a completely valid test for unethical behavior. I have a college friend, for example, who has made hundreds of millions of dollars through a legitimate business idea. He has given away many millions to worthy causes over the years under the cloak of total anonymity. Certainly, his acts are totally ethical despite his unwillingness to publicize them. It is valid, however, to assume that if we do not want others to know what we have done; we should reconsider whether or not our actions were right.

If it is important that others not know what you are doing, it might be an indication that what you are doing is wrong.

21

WHAT IF EVERYBODY DID WHAT I HAVE DONE?

We owe the seventh test for ethical thought to the great German philosopher Immanuel Kant (1724–1804). In his words, we should ***"Act only according to that maxim whereby you can at the same time will that it should become a universal law."*** Simply put; "What if everybody did it?" For example, in the case of lying, what if everybody believed that lying was acceptable behavior and did it with abandon? Business would fall apart. Despite perceptions to the contrary, business still operates largely on the basis of trust. We trust our vendors to deliver on time and to maintain the quality we have specified. We trust contractors to do quality work. We trust our guests to act civilly as guests and to not take the towels with them when they check out. Yes, there are exceptions, but, by and large, guests are honest. What if everyone broke the law whenever they could? There are not enough policemen in the world to control such situations. Most people realize that following the law benefits everyone, and they do so. People, and this is especially true of Americans, go out of their way not to hurt others. When a catastrophe such as 9-11 happens, Americans open their hearts and their wallets. What if no one cared if they hurt others or not? Who would want to live in such an environment?

Does this apply to Vanessa in our cocktail lounge? It certainly does. What if, suddenly, we are discovered as being tolerant to prostitution almost to the extent of encouraging it? If that were to become the prime focus of our cocktail lounge, we would soon be on the phone to law enforcement, asking them to clean up the situation for us. What makes Vanessa's situation tolerable to management is that it is a contained event that has not caused anyone in the hotel any trouble. Once more Vanessa's appear, however, the situation will quickly grow out of control. And more Vanessa's are inevitable if the situation is left alone.

If what you are deciding would not work as a universal decision, it has a high probability of being unethical.

22

AN OVERVIEW OF VANESSA

To the strict moralist, the situation of Vanessa working the cocktail lounge is clearly a case of illegal prostitution and must not be allowed to happen. To the realist, however, the situation as described is not so clear cut. Instead of Vanessa, assume that we are discussing Mary Widow, who stops by for a drink, meets a compatible gentleman, and travels with him to his room, where no money trades hands. Management cannot deny Mary the right to be in the cocktail lounge alone, nor to make the acquaintance of a gentleman. There is nothing illegal about her visiting her friend in his room. If she spends the night, there could be an issue of single versus double occupancy, but if she does not spend the night, that issue is moot. Management really has no right to inject itself into that situation. With regard to Vanessa, the difference is that money is exchanged, changing the scenario from intimate friendship to prostitution. The problem is one of proof and one of complaint. If the money passing is not witnessed and no one is willing to complain, there is little in the way of a prosecutable case. This makes Vanessa's case very difficult for management, but that hardly makes it right. We have surveyed many managers and department heads on this exact scenario and, invariably, 70% say that they would not involve themselves in the situation. There is a saying in management that no situation is static; either it gets better or it gets worse. Our scenario cannot get better as long as Vanessa is working our cocktail lounge. Eventually, Vanessa will bring a friend, or other working girls will discover her playground. There is always the possibility that organized crime will enter in, and drugs are always a threat. When and if the situation becomes serious, it is not going to be helpful if it can be shown that management was fully aware of the situation and did nothing to correct it: Without accusation, management should discretely ask Vanessa to ply her trade elsewhere, and if that does not work, they should seek help from law enforcement. Unfortunately, in many situations like this, “Vanessa” has already compromised one or more members of management, making correction even more difficult. The bottom line of this discussion is that it is always best to put water on the embers of ethical misconduct because embers can fan into uncontrollable flames. Once an ethical situation is identified, however convenient it may be to simply ignore it, ignoring it is not the proper solution.

Ignoring small, non threatening ethical dilemmas often leads to being confronted with major difficult dilemmas.

23

THE VALUE OF ETHICS

Why be ethical? More to the point and more to the manager's thinking, "Will being ethical pay?" Perhaps the best answer to this question can be found in the work of James E. Burke, CEO of Johnson & Johnson (J&J) from 1976 to 1989, and his mentor, General Robert Wood Johnson, who founded J&J in 1940. It all began when Johnson created his now-famous corporate credo.

Our Credo

We believe our first responsibility is to the doctors, nurses and patients,
to mothers and fathers and all others who use our products and services.
In meeting their needs everything we do must be of high quality.
We must constantly strive to reduce our costs
in order to maintain reasonable prices.
Customers' orders must be serviced promptly and accurately.
Our suppliers and distributors must have an opportunity
to make a fair profit.

We are responsible to our employees,
the men and women who work with us throughout the world.
Everyone must be considered as an individual.
We must respect their dignity and recognize their merit.
They must have a sense of security in their jobs.
Compensation must be fair and adequate,
and working conditions clean, orderly and safe.
We must be mindful of ways to help our employees fulfill
their family responsibilities.
Employees must feel free to make suggestions and complaints.
There must be equal opportunity for employment, development
and advancement for those qualified.
We must provide competent management,
and their actions must be just and ethical.

We are responsible to the communities in which we live and work
and to the world community as well.
We must be good citizens — support good works and charities
and bear our fair share of taxes.
We must encourage civic improvements and better health and education.
We must maintain in good order
the property we are privileged to use,
protecting the environment and natural resources.

Our final responsibility is to our stockholders.
Business must make a sound profit.
We must experiment with new ideas.
Research must be carried on, innovative programs developed
and mistakes paid for.
New equipment must be purchased, new facilities provided
and new products launched.
Reserves must be created to provide for adverse times.
When we operate according to these principles,
the stockholders should realize a fair return.

Johnson & Johnson

The credo placed the customer first, before the shareholders, on the theory that taking care of the customer would result in profits that would ultimately satisfy the shareholders. Willard Marriott had a similar approach in the more labor intensive hotel industry when he said, *"Take care of the employees, and they will take care of the guests.*" When Burke took over as Chief Operating Officer of J&J in 1976, he questioned whether or not General Johnson's credo was being internalized enough by the J&J employees to really be effective. Of course, it was hanging on the wall of virtually every J&J office worldwide, but that alone did not mean that it was both understood and implemented. Burke called 24 of his managers together for a meeting to challenge the credo. What he discovered was that the credo was a set of guidelines far more powerful than he had ever imagined. Burke followed up with a series of credo challenging meetings around the world, resulting in some rewording of the credo without any change to the basic philosophy. Burke then began a study to answer the question "Does being an ethical corporation pay?" He and his staff assembled a list of 26 Fortune 500 companies that had uninterrupted 30-year track records of practicing ethical management. Upon further examination, they dropped 11 of the 26 from the list for various reasons. Some had had small interruptions during the 30 years. Some were dropped because they had no stockholders, and others, like McDonalds, had strong track records for their lifetimes but had lifetimes that fell short of 30 years. When Burke examined the 15 remaining companies, he found that they had enjoyed a compounded rate of profits of 11%, which was 3 times greater than the Gross National Product, which had grown 3.1% over the same period. Burke determined that if, 30 years before, someone had invested $30,000 in a composite of the Dow Jones, that person would have been worth $134,000 at the end of 30 years, a gain of $104,000. If the person had invested $30,000 ($2000 each) in the 15 companies with solid track records in ethics, however, that person would have been worth $1,021,861 at the end of the same 30-year period, a gain of $991,861. This represents a profit of more than 9 times greater than that of the Dow composite. Burke concluded that ethics really does pay.

In September of 1982, tragedy struck J&J. Someone had laced Tylenol, the nation's leading over-the-counter pain medication, with cyanide, causing the death of seven Chicago area residents. Immediately, it was universally believed that these incidents spelled the death of Tylenol, but James Burke and his J&J team were ready.

According to the Encyclopedia of Management,

"Rather than trying to cover up the story, Burke quickly put out the word across the media, even appearing on several television programs. He warned the public to avoid all Tylenol products until the company had more information about the tampering."

Johnson & Johnson quickly recalled some 31 million bottles of Tylenol—about one hundred million dollars worth of product. Within six weeks Burke had devised a plan to put tamper-proof packaging on all Tylenol products. His bold move restored customer confidence. Just one year after the cyanide lacing tragedy, Tylenol had regained most of its previous market share.

When tainted Tylenol resurfaced a few years later, Burke decided to do away with capsules entirely. Despite the fact that his decision cost the company as much as $150 million,

Burke said at a press conference, “we owe it to customers” (Time, March 3, 1986).

James E. Burke has received many honors, chief among them the Presidential Medal of Freedom. He was also named one of the “Ten Greatest CEOs of All Time” by *Fortune* magazine in 2002.

Placing the customer first and practicing ethics at every level of the organization will pay great dividends for the company.

24

EXAMPLES OF ETHICAL ISSUES

In the 2006 survey of U. S. hotels over 300 rooms, Department heads were asked to suggest examples of ethical misconduct relating to their departments. Here follows a listing of the most frequent responses

ID	ETHICAL ISSUE	AFFECTED PROPERTY
1	Using contractors for personal use	Company profits
2	Sharing bids with favorite vendor	Company profits
3	Upgrades for cash tips	Company image
4	Specifying noncompetitive brands	Company profits
5	Accepting gifts for reduced rates	Company profits
6	Hidden commissions to third parties	Company profits

7	Guests who fabricate complaints	Company profits
8	Employees badmouthing organization	Company image
9	Meeting planner wrongly blaming hotel	Company image
10	Guest wrongly demanding compensation	Company profits
11	Price fixing	Customer financial
12	Applicant falsifying information	Company image
13	Sales Manager creating bogus contracts	Company profits
14	False worker comp claims	Company profits
15	Falsifying leaves or absences	Company profits
16	Overcharging guests	Customer financial
17	Advertising undeliverable services	Customer financial
18	Improper security precautions	Consumer safety
19	Entertaining "friends" on expense account	Company profits
20	Married manager dating	Company image
21	Nondisclosure of conflict of interest	Company profits
22	Pouring heavy or free drinks	Company profits

23	Stealing food products	Company profits
24	Not turning in found valuables	Customer financial
25	Cooking books	Government financial
26	Taking confiscated property	Company image
27	Selling free products to employees	Employee financial
28	Cheating on time sheets	Company profits
29	Stealing personal guest info for fraud	Customer financial
30	Favoritism in salaries and bonuses	Employee financial
31	Improper relationship with staff	Company image
32	Nepotism	Company image
33	Gossiping about guests and co-workers	Individual image
34	Differential treatment of employees	Individual image
35	Giving out confidential information	Individual image
36	Bad mouthing competition to customers	Company image
37	Inadequate maintenance.	Property image
38	Purposely overcharging	Customer financial

39	Not honoring contracts with guest and suppliers	Customer financial
40	Rate discussions with competitors	Customer financial
41	Unauthorized rates given to clients	Company profits
42	Denying cancels due to a disaster	Customer financial
43	Purchasing without competitive bidding	Company profits
44	Allowing unauthorized entrance	Company profits
45	Overcharging on consumption events	Customer financial
46	Misappropriation of company assets	Company profits
47	Illegal substances in the workplace	Company image
48	Invoice fraud	Company profits
49	Under-recording liabilities	Shareholder financial
50	Enforcing safety measures	Employee/ Customer safety
51	Discussing rate-setting with competitors	Customer financial
52	Unfair compensation for women and minorities	Employee financial
53	Balance-sheet inaccuracy	Government financial
54	Price fixing	Customer financial

55	Overvaluing—Misrepresenting Pro Forma	Lender's financial
56	Bait-and-switch advertising	Consumer financial
57	Substituting less than advertised quality	Consumer financial
58	Failure to update safety inspections	Consumer safety

The list, albeit incomplete, indicates that there are many areas of ethical impropriety in the hospitality industry and, further, that property is indicated in every instance. If the element of trust is to be maintained with the consumer, it is necessary for the industry to address the issue of ethics at all levels.

The Hospitality Industry needs to increase its focus on ethical issues to maintain consumer trust.

25

WRITING A CODE OF ETHICS

A meaningful code of ethics is the moral compass of the organization. Codes always begin at the uppermost level of the organization, which, by necessity, are broad in scope. Although considerable thought must go into each code statement, the process of producing a meaningful code is not difficult. Fundamentally, because communication of the code throughout the organization is paramount, the code must be clear, concise, and in writing. We will analyze a general code for the service and tourism industry as a whole with the caveat that it represents one approach and is not intended to be equally acceptable to all. This is because a code represents the philosophy and direction of the creator and not all persons agree on relative importance. For example, there are quite different views as to the treatment of employees. We favor the approach taken by Willard Marriott, who is quoted as saying, "Take care of your employees and they will take care of your guests." A more traditional view, however, is that production-level employees must be micromanaged, high turnover is inevitable, and strict supervision is the only way to ensure a quality product. There may well be two different approaches to an ethic regarding the treatment of employees.

The first step in creating a code is to identify the major tasks to be achieved at the level under consideration. For the industry, they could be:

Recognizing the overall desire to manage in an ethical fashion.

Maintaining the image and reputation of the overall industry.

Focusing on self-improvement and refraining from denigrating those outside your organization.

Treating all guests equally.

Delivering a product and service with total consistency.

Ensuring the safety and health of all guests and employees.

Being an organization that promotes trust and honesty at all levels for guests, employees, and the public.

Doing whatever is required to facilitate the performance of employees.

Treating all employees equally and fairly.

Not doing anything that would damage the environment in which you work.

Earning a meaningful profit that is fair and honest.

This list is not intended to be exclusive or complete. It is, however, a good start at identifying those general elements that will produce a high element of trust in the service and tourism industry. The code of ethics for such a list of management principles might look as follows:

CODE OF ETHICS
SERVICE AND TOURISM INDUSTRY

1. We acknowledge ethics and morality as inseparable elements of doing business and we will test every decision against the highest standards of honesty, legality, fairness, impunity and conscience.

2. We will conduct ourselves at all times, personally and collectively, so as to bring credit to the service and tourism industry at large.

3. We will concentrate our time, energy and resources on the improvement of our own product and services and we will not denigrate our competition in the pursuit of our own success.

4. We will treat all guests equally regardless of race, religion, nationality, creed or sex.

5. We will deliver all standards of service and product with total consistency to each and every guest.

6. We will provide a totally safe and sanitary environment at all times to every guest and employee.

7. We will, in words and deeds, develop and maintain the highest level of trust, honesty and understanding among guests, employees, employers and the public at large.

8. We will provide every employee, at every level, all of the knowledge, training, equipment and motivation required to perform his or her tasks according to our published standards.

9. We will guarantee that every employee at all levels, engaged in the same or similar tasks, will have the same opportunity to perform and advance, and will be evaluated against the same standards.

10. We will actively and conscientiously work to protect and preserve our environment and natural resource in all that we do.

11. We will seek a fair and honest profit, no more, and no less.

Within the framework of the overall code, the company would produce a code in the same fashion, reflecting the company philosophy followed by the respective divisions within the company and the departments within the divisions.

Codes of ethics can also be written for individuals using the same approach. A personal code of ethics might look as follows:

PERSONAL ETHICS

"I shall, from this day on, seek the right way of living and accept personal responsibility for everything that I do, from which will flow the balance that will enrich both my values and those of my environment."

- Respect the right of others to legally own and benefit from their personal property

- Live ethically and morally at all times and possess the strength of character to be proactive in the pursuit of right.

- Tolerate all ethical beliefs and ideologies as the guiding force in my commitment to practice truth and non-violence.

- Treat all individuals fairly and objectively at all times.

- Commit to the constant nurturing of an environment in which others can achieve their maximum potential for excellence

- Act rightly not because we have virtue or excellence; but we rather have these because we act rightly.

- Constantly seek to improve the fundamental personal values that provide the direction, strength and character of my actions.

- Seek the positive reinforcement that comes from the highest ideals and values of those around me.

- Grow from the power of helping others achieve their highest level of moral and ethical aspiration.

(IIQEST 1998)

A meaningful code of ethics is the moral compass of the organization and the individuals therein.

IMPLEMENTING THE PROGRAM

26

ASSEMBLING THE TEAM

The fundamental first step in the implementation process is having the commitment from the topmost executive in the organization. In a chain, that means the President, the corporate suite, and the Board of Directors. Total commitment means a commitment of time and financial resources. It means strong support for those charged with the development and management of the program. And it means a total dedication to the philosophy so that employees at all levels want to pursue excellence and will do so if given the right tools, training, and support to do the job. Unless top management is totally committed to excellence, a program should not be initiated, because it is doomed to failure. Once commitment is present, a leader at the corporate level should be chosen. This individual will have the responsibility to oversee and guide the program throughout the organization. The Director of Excellence must be chosen with careful thought. Someone should not (as I have witnessed in several situations) be picked just because of seniority or because he or she has time available because of light responsibilities in his or her regular job. The position requires great energy and enthusiasm. It requires someone who can command the respect of the team he or she is charged to lead. It requires someone with political awareness. For example, the Director of Excellence will become a respected leader among the employees at all levels, but the role of the Director of Excellence is that of administering the program within the framework of the corporate and unit management, and the director must be savvy enough to stay within the bounds of political correctness. There will be many occasions to enter into discussions of wages and benefits, for example, but that is to be avoided, as such issues are the purview of top management and not of the Director of Excellence.

The task of Director of Excellence is not a full-time job except in a very large property, where it may become so at the discretion of management. Primary responsibilities involve promoting the excellence program, working through the Committee for Excellence as the Chair, and overseeing the management and progress of the overall effort.

Once the Director of Excellence is designated from the staff, the next step is to select the Committee for Excellence. Three members will suffice in a small operation of 100 rooms or less, and 5 members will suffice for larger operations. Members should be Department Heads. The committee will meet for 1 hour per week. It is important to remember at this point that the Journey to Excellence is an ongoing program, not a one-shot quick fix. The program is a change in company mentality from Excellence by dictate to Excellence by dedication and commitment. It doesn't happen overnight. Be patient, working slowly and deliberately, making certain that each step is implemented correctly before moving on.

The committee meets at a regularly scheduled time for one hour each week. The temptation to meet for more than one hour should be overcome. Once up and running, the primary work of the program happens at the production and supervisory levels; thus, the role of the committee is to oversee the program, and one hour per week is sufficient. The idea that work expands to fill the time available is significant in my mind. Permitting the committee to work in an unlimited time frame does not seem to produce more and better output but, rather, more words and more frustration in that the discipline to bring closure to a task is removed. The essence of a successful Program for Excellence is to continuously make small but significant improvements, not to develop and implement a program in the shortest time. Avoid burnout by keeping the pace slow but productive and steady.

Appoint someone on the Committee for Excellence to serve as Vice Director to lead in the absence of the Director of Excellence. Appoint another to serve as secretary. Avoid lengthy minutes. The heart of the program rests in the development of standards, not in who said what, when, and why. The information in the minutes should be limited to only a few things:

- Date and time of meeting
- Members and guests present
- Action areas identified
- Action taken
- Time of adjournment

Most times, the minutes can be written on a single page. Members of the Committee for Excellence should serve on staggered terms to maintain continuity and to keep the committee fresh and vibrant.

A successful program for excellence results from a committed top management working through a qualified director who supervises and motivates a dedicated committee.

27

STARTING THE JOURNEY TO EXCELLENCE

The first action of the Committee for Excellence is to assemble and fine-tune the job descriptions of every position in the organization. This exercise alone will highlight what we call "job-title creep," in which we discover that many titles are created to differentiate individuals when, in fact, the actual job is no different from others performing basically the same functions. The philosophy to follow is to keep the same job title for all employees doing the same tasks. In this process and the one to follow (identifying job tasks), it is important to involve Department Heads and Supervisors because they are best equipped to understand the nature and responsibilities of all job titles under their supervision. Once a fine-tuned list of job titles has been developed, the committee now turns to developing a body of tasks for each job title. This is not a listing of what each person does. It is an identification of broad areas of responsibility. A Department Head, for example, checks employee performance, implements corrections, disciplines, rewards, motivates, hears grievances, and so on, but all of these actions come under the task of supervising subordinates.

If you identify more than 8 tasks for any job title, you have probably been too specific and need to review the tasks and consolidate them. A waitress, for example would have the following tasks:

- Report for duty
- Set up work area
- Greet and seat guests
- Take orders
- Serve guests
- Conclude the transaction
- Check-out and depart

Everything the waitress does can fit within one of these tasks. The same philosophy applies to every job title at every level from General Manager to houseman.

It is absolutely crucial that Department Heads and Supervisors develop the job tasks. Not only are they the best suited to perform the function, they must become intimately involved in the Journey to Excellence early on. Department Heads and Supervisors will ultimately control the success of the program because they will monitor the compliance to the standards that result from the tasks. There is the temptation in the service and tourism industry for top management to believe that they alone must set the standards, but because Department Heads and Supervisors are not involved, they often misrepresent the monitoring process and destroy the program's effectiveness.

Use any word-processing program such as WordPerfect or Microsoft Word to create an outline of job titles and tasks. Organize the outline by departments and sub-departments. This is important because you will be printing out and distributing to each department each year a list of titles, tasks, and standards for review and revision.

Once the job tasks have been identified and listed, the committee now turns to the effort of answering the question "In what area are we having the greatest difficulty?" Let's assume that you are encountering long lines at check-out. By analyzing the problem, perhaps some pre-check–out standards can be implemented. Beyond that, the situation calls for cross-training such that someone is triggered to step into the check-out process when the situation calls for intervention (i.e., the lines exceed management's predetermined standard). A standard is created to address the situation. Assistant Managers are the obvious candidates to intervene, but they are not the only ones. Someone in proximity to the front desk, such as a bookkeeper or the auditor, could be pressed into action. Have you ever been in a long discount store checkout line when someone opened a new register and said, "I can help someone over here?" We are all very appreciative when that happens. It indicates genuine concern for the shopper's positive attitude.

Permit me to cite two very simple examples of basic standards that affect excellence. I experienced both. Mervie, a Scandinavian student of mine studying at a top European hotel school, was hired by a prominent US hotel chain for a summer job. At the end of her first day, Mervie was totally frustrated and discouraged. She had been placed on the front desk with no real training. She knew check-in and check-out procedures and could speak 5 languages fluently. What she did not know were the answers to questions such as "How do I get to the museum? What time do the subways stop running? Is there a drugstore close by?" The obvious standard would be for the hotel to develop a list of the frequently asked questions, which new front desk hires would be required to study and pass a test on before starting their jobs.

In another case, this time in the Bahamas, the General Manager, having lunch on the veranda, said to me, "Watch the waitress serving those guests. What she will do is driving me crazy." Sure enough, the waitress brought the food to the table of 5 and said, holding a plate, "Who ordered the chicken salad sandwich?" She proceeded to ask a similar question for the next 3 plates. "Why can't she remember who ordered what?" he asked. The answer is that no one ever taught her to take the orders by starting, for example, with "the lady in the red dress" and going clockwise around the table, which would allow her to get the orders right without asking.

Readers will agree that these two examples are very minor in nature, but we must remember that excellence is taking the very minor acts of service and performing them flawlessly every time.

When developing standards, remember to filter them for their ethical content first. Before you develop the standard to add exorbitant telephone surcharges to guests' bills, you may want to explore the ultimate consequences regarding the ethics of your action.

Finally, be cautioned that true excellence will not result from writing a myriad of standards and then demanding compliance. This is called "forced adoption" (to be discussed further on), and it does not work. True excellence results from implementing carefully crafted standards slowly and deliberately at a pace that permits them to be fully absorbed and executed flawlessly every time. Slower is decidedly better in implementing standards because employees develop pride in compliance with this approach, whereas excessive speed often results in frustration and discontent.

A successful Program for Excellence is a slow, deliberative process of constant improvement, allowing employees to absorb standards and implement them to perfection with total consistency.

28

HANDLING THE A-TYPICAL STANDARD

Thus far, we have concentrated on writing basic standards in a concise, clear manner so they are unambiguous and easily understood and implemented by the employee. Not all standards, however, lend themselves to such simplicity. For example, every property has a procedure for the fire emergency. Such procedures are generally written up as comprehensive plans of action covering all employees. Parts of the plan can be extracted and used as simple one-sentence standards for individual job tasks. For example, ***"Every employee must report the instance of a fire immediately by calling ______."*** This is absolutely essential and can be communicated in easy, clear, objective terms. But what about the use of a fire extinguisher? This is a separate training process and essential to the overall safety of the guests. As such, a standard is required, but the result would be many standards to communicate the total process. This would defeat the purpose of the standards-writing process because it would add too much verbiage to communicate what is better done by a different approach.

Another example of an A-typical standard is the employee handbook. All employees need to know what is contained therein, but the handbook does not lend itself to a multitude of individual standards.

In the two examples, it is suggested that every employee have at least two simple standards. First, "Read and be familiar with the fire emergency handbook dated _______ and take and pass a course on the use of fire extinguishers" Second, "Read and be familiar with the employee handbook dated ______." Then, of course is the responsibility of setting up well-organized periodic training programs for both subjects.

There are many other areas that lend themselves to the same approach. For example, there is the question of how to interact and communicate with physically challenged guests and employees. There is the subject of a code of ethics for the organization. Also, there are procedures to follow when there is an issue of guest injury or death. In housekeeping, there are precise standards for making the bed that best lend themselves to a diagram or video training process. The set-up for the guest amenity basket is also an example of a process better communicated by a photo than by a multitude of standards.

A-typical standards are best handled by one standard directing the subject to a broader training process.

29

WORKING WITH THE UNION

Over the years, I have conducted several studies in which general managers were asked to rate several industries on their practice of ethics. Almost without exception, managers rated unions at the lowest level. No studies have been done in which union officials were asked to rate hotels, but the odds are fairly high that they would rate them low as well. The point is that relationships with the union begin with distrust and ill perceptions, not a good environment for meaningful progress. From the union side, the perception will be that by eliminating errors, the hotel can reduce the labor force and, of course, this is a union red flag. In actuality, the reverse is true. By eliminating errors, occupancy will improve, which often results in the need to increase staff. It is a fact that consumers will pay more for dependable excellence, thus improving bottom-line profits. Increased profits means the ability to pay higher wages. Increased hiring and the potential for increased wages are both highly valued by the union. Although committing to the possibilities is something that hotels should not do, acknowledging the positive potential for a program for excellence is the best way to obtain the attention of the union and gain, if not their immediate support, at least gain their willingness to cooperate. Another aspect of the relationship is the complaint by unions that management often manages by dictate, criticizing employees for not performing up to standards that have not been properly communicated to the employee. The excellence program presented in this book addresses this factor in two ways. By having employees included in the development of standards and by properly recording standards in written form, communication is vastly improved, and when standards are not met, there is little argument as to what the deficiency is. Further, a successful program for excellence builds employee pride, which results in heightened job satisfaction and less complaining. Union officials can therefore concentrate on union–management relationships in properties without successful programs, thus relieving the pressure from the successful program.

A good start would be for management to meet with the union early on and discuss the program and the anticipated results. Done properly, this will result in union acceptance, and although skepticism will still prevail, it will soon be overcome by success. Management should be aware, however, that once the Journey to Excellence proves to be a success, the union will insist that such a program be implemented elsewhere, often by your competitors. Some managers will view this as undesirable, but such a view is shortsighted. It is far better to be the leader and have others rushing to catch up than to be the follower and be forced into action. Plus, by encouraging others to pursue programs of excellence, the destination will attract more attention and more business. Convention cities are a good illustration of destination excellence. Convention sites are selected based on evaluation of facilities, to be sure, but the overall appeal of the city is also important. A city's overall appeal is a function of excellent restaurants, excellent transportation, excellent sightseeing attractions, and a strong welcoming attitude on the part of the city tourism organizers. Being the best facility in a city that is deficient in overall attractiveness is not a good bottom line, whereas being part of overall excellence is. Unions can understand the value of excellence if it is patiently explained to them, and this effort is well worth pursuing early on in the program.

Bringing the union on board early on is a necessary step in a successful Journey to Excellence program.

DIFFUSION

30

DIFFUSION—A HELPFUL TOOL

While studying for my MBA at Michigan State University, I had the distinct pleasure of studying under Dr. Everett Rogers, who is a pioneer in the subject of diffusion of ideas and innovations.[1] Diffusion is the process of causing a social system to adopt an idea it perceives as new. The course was fascinating in that Dr. Rogers and others researched those elements of human nature that encourage and/or resist the adoption of new ideas. Much of what we do in life is governed by the principles of diffusion. I have personally used the principles of the adoption process to win public office, build successful organizations, conduct fundraising campaigns, and implement the Quest for Quality program in the American Hotel and Motel Association. I also employed the techniques when serving as Quality Assurance Director at ITT-Sheraton Worldwide. The relevance that diffusion has for our Journey to Excellence is that the program is often perceived by those affected as a new idea. For our journey to be successful, it is important that we know something about diffusion. According to Rogers, there are 5 steps in the process of adopting a new idea:

[1] See, for example, *Communication of Innovation* by Dr. Everett M. Rogers and Floyd Shoemaker, The Free Press, New York, 1971.

1 **AWARENESS**—The individual learns of the existence of a new idea but lacks information about it.

2 **INTEREST**—The individual develops interest in the innovation and seeks additional information about it.

3 **EVALUATION**—The individual makes a mental application of the new idea to his present and anticipated future situation and evaluates whether or not to try it.

4 **TRIAL**—The individual applies the new idea on a small scale to determine the utility in his or her own situation

5 **ADOPTION**—The individual uses the new idea continuously on a full scale.

Assume that the new idea is the purchase of an automobile. Our car is 6 years old and encountering more frequent repairs. We are aware that it may be time to buy new. Advertising piques our interest and, after visiting several showrooms, we decide that a particular model appeals to us. We evaluate our financial situation and our transportation utility needs and head for the dealership. We listen to the salesman and then try out the car in a test drive. We then decide to buy the car.

There are 2 issues relating to the adoption stage that are critical to our Journey to Excellence. First, let us assume that some employees do not adopt the idea of the Journey to Excellence program. Further, let us assume that our program is well underway and a potential guest does not adopt the idea that we provide first-class excellence. In both cases, although we have been rejected, it is not fatal, by any means. It simply means that we have not provided sufficient motivation. Or it means that the motivation is there but the individual is simply not yet ready to change. If we are confident that our product is correct, we simply forge ahead, and, eventually, adoption will take place. From another approach, assume adaption has taken place. The adopters now have expectations relating to their decision to adopt, expectations that we have created in our persuasion process. If those expectations are not met, we have what is known as discontinuance. The adopter simply gives up and abandons our innovation. This is vastly worse than initially being rejected in that it will be almost impossible to regain the discontinued individual. Bottom line, don't begin the Journey to Excellence unless you are totally committed to doing it correctly at every phase. Discontinuance must be avoided at all costs.

Now let us put the shoe on the other foot and explore those issues that cause us to accept a new idea. There are again 5 elements that people examine when confronted with a new idea that they are being asked to adopt:

RELATIVE ADVANTAGE—Better known as WIFM ("What's in it for me?"), relative advantage asks to what degree the innovation is perceived as being better than the idea it supersedes

COMPATIBILITY—The innovation must be perceived as compatible with the participant's existing values, needs, and experiences.

COMPLEXITY—The innovation must be perceived as relatively easy to understand and put into practice.

TRIALABILITY—The innovation must be able to be tried, even if only on a limited basis.

OBSERVABILITY—The results of the innovation must be visible and readily interpreted.

If the Journey to Excellence is communicated as eliminating errors and thereby reducing wasted labor costs, you are defeated before you start because employees will interpret it as a productivity program aimed at cutting back staff. If, however, the program is perceived as a basically simple program aimed at making the employees' job easier while increasing guest satisfaction, it is well on the way to acceptance. It is good to consider these elements in all communications about the program to minimize any negative perceptions.

Excellence is an idea perceived by many to be new; understanding the principles of adoption facilitates the process of implementation.

31

ADOPTER CATEGORIES AND THE DIFFUSION PROCESS

Rogers has identified and codified 5 categories of adopters that are important in our knowledge of the diffusion process:

INNOVATORS—(2.5% of the diffusion population)—VENTURESOME

EARLY ADOPTERS—(13.5%)—RESPECT ROLE

EARLY MAJORITY—(34%)—DELIBERATE

LATE MAJORITY—(34%)—SKEPTICAL

LAGGARDS—(16%)—TRADITIONAL

INNOVATORS (I) —It is easy to become excited by those who adopt the excellence program quickly and enthusiastically, but excitement about this is an error of perception. Innovators are eager to jump on any new idea and do so often without adequate thought. Research has found that innovators lack true staying power and that if a new idea comes along or if questions arise, they are equally quick to abandon their initial acceptance. Although innovators are important as an encouraging sign of adoption, they should not be regarded as a sound foundation of the process.

EARLY ADOPTERS (EA) —This group is more stable than the innovators and form the foundation for growth as they adopt the Journey to Excellence program. They have given the idea real thought and concluded that it is in their best interest to join. They are eager to participate and have their decision reinforced by recognition. OPINION LEADERS (to be discussed later) usually come from the early-adopter group. To put the adoption process into perspective (somewhat nebulous because all adoption processes vary somewhat), a property of 300 employees will have approximately 8 innovators and 40 early adopters. Thus, when 48 employees sign onto the program, it is a sign that the process is gaining momentum.

EARLY MAJORITY (EM) —This group has more of a follower mentality than a leadership mentality, but they do indicate a solid acceptance of the adoption. In our 300-employee example, when 150, or 50%, have signed on, a successful process is well in sight.

LATE MAJORITY (LM) —This group represents the greatest challenge to the program. They have been skeptical from the start, and although they are encouraged by the existing adopters, they must be persuaded to join in, or their reticence will have a negative impact on those who have already adopted. Investing time and energy in communicating the commitment and enthusiasm of those who have adopted will be most helpful in encouraging the late majority.

LAGGARDS (L)—This is a bothersome group and will represent some 48 or so of our 300 employees. Some will never adopt the program, and others will do so most reluctantly. The important message for management is that laggards are an inevitable part of all adoption programs in whatever numbers and should not occupy an inordinate amount of management time. They will eventually adopt or leave the organization, both beneficial results.

If we were to plot the adopter categories in a bar graph, it would somewhat resemble a normal distribution curve.

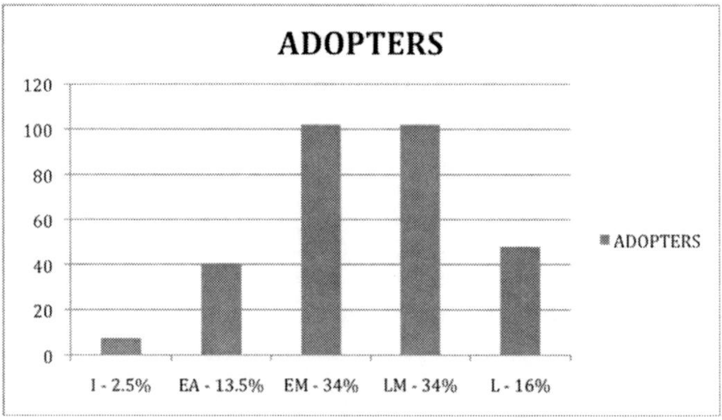

If we were to plot the categories cumulatively over time, we would have a typical "S" curve.

Adopter Categories

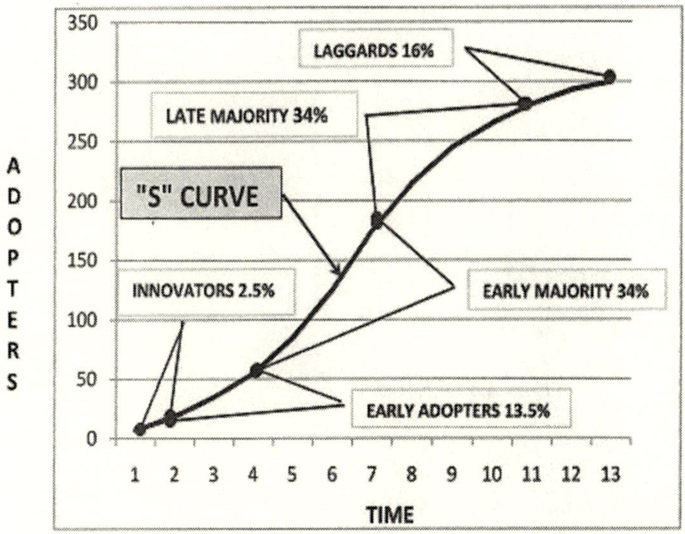

Everything in life follows an “S” curve; everything has a beginning and an end. The curve will vary depending on time and conditions, but everything has this basic “S” curve depicting its life cycle. Hopefully, our Journey to Excellence program has a long and productive life.

When the property utilizing the program ceases to be economically feasible, however, the property will end, and along with it, our program. This cannot always be avoided. What we want to avoid, however, is a premature end (i.e., a failed program once adopted).

Let us now turn to the steps in the adoption process.

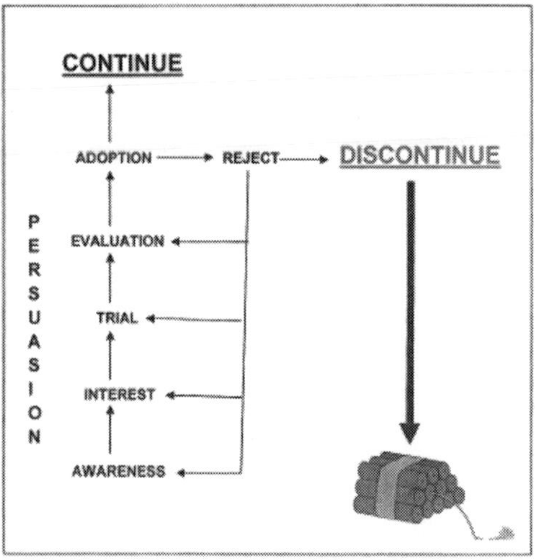

DIFFUSION ADOPTER STEPS

The above chart is key to understanding the adoption process for our Journey to Excellence program and to the basic life cycle of all adoption processes. First, note that Rogers has grouped the steps of interest, trial, and evaluation steps into a general category called “persuasion.” This is because these 3 steps do not always occur in the sequence shown. Sometimes evaluation precedes trial, and sometimes interest does not peak before evaluation. “Persuasion” simplifies the communication. We will stick with the 4 steps leading in “order” to adoption because each is important, regardless of the order it happens in relations to the others.

Employees are made aware of the impending Journey to Excellence program largely through mass media, that is, the company newsletter or individual notices. Their interest is generated by communication of the relative advantage, compatibility, complexity, trialability, and observability of the program. Understanding the needs of the receivers of the communications will permit you to answer employee questions before they are asked. In other words, management should resist simply announcing a new program; rather, they should tell the employees what advantages the program will have for them, the employees, when implemented. The Journey to Excellence program will make for more satisfied guests, increase business, encourage larger tips, permit higher wages, and generate pride. It will also, of course, increase profits, but employees are not motivated by higher profits unless the higher profits will eventually benefit them. If you communicate with the employees' receptivity in mind, the program is more readily adopted.

Interest will come as employees see the commitment from management and begin to understand the benefits to them.

As already discussed, the best approach to excellence is not a massive application but rather a slow, deliberate approach. This will permit employees to try out the elements by implementing a new standard and mastering it before moving on to the next standard. Remember, one does not learn to play the piano by starting with a Mozart symphony. Rather, the student learns by starting with scales and simple songs until he or she grows in skill and confidence. The same is true with the Journey to Excellence installation. Help employees to master small steps before you introduce larger ones.

Evaluation is an ongoing process leading either to rejection of the program or adoption of it. Should rejection occur, it is not fatal. It simply means that the employee has not yet been fully convinced that the program merits acceptance. Continued trial, interest, and evaluation will eventually lead to adoption.

A word about forced adoption: While implementing a program in a prominent, beach front Caribbean resort property, I was informed by the Executive Assistant Manager, "Quality. I will tell you how to get quality: I tell them (the employees) what to do, and they do it or I fire them!" This is classic forced adoption, and although it might work initially, it will surely fail eventually. This resort hotel did not implement the program, and the property eventually went bankrupt.

A major point to remember is that all adoption processes are motivated by expectations. Assume that we have communicated our Journey to Excellence program successfully, employees have adopted it, and employees' expectations are established. If those expectations are met, adoption continues. If not, we have what is called discontinuance, which is fatal. Should discontinuance occur, the employee is lost—if not forever, at least for a long time. For example, one major restaurant chain has spectacular product advertising, but the actual product never equals the advertised one. I went there twice but will go no more because my expectations were not met.

The discontinuance issue is one reason that it is not good to overstate your product or claim to have excellence. Doing so tends to make the adopters skeptical and cause them to be watchful for unmet expectations.

It is always best for the adopters to recognize excellence on their own and freely communicate their pleasure in that excellence to others.

Individuals adopt new ideas in predictable ways that, when understood, facilitate the adoption process.

32

OPINION LEADERS

In the process of applying the principles of diffusion to the Journey to Excellence, no concept is more valuable than that of opinion leaders. Diffusion is primarily a communication process: communicating the value of the program, communicating standards to the employees, communicating the goodwill to the guests and customers, and so on. Communicating is a somewhat simple process but for one element: Proper communication requires a meaningful feedback process to be effective. Without the feedback process, we do not know if and how our message was received. Often, lack of action regarding a communication is attributed to apathy on the part of the receiver when, in fact, it is often the fault of the sender and the message sent. Feedback is the only way that we know that the proper message was received and understood. One of the most important messages in the Journey to Excellence implementation process is how the program is being received. Most managers believe that we simply ask the employees and they will set us straight, but such an approach is not always effective. Many employees will tend to tell us what we want to hear whether or not it is accurate feedback. How, then, do we acquire good feedback information? This is where the opinion leaders come in.

If we could somehow look down on our organization for several days and plot the interactions that take place between employees, we would discover that some employees have far more interactions than the rest. These individuals are the opinion leaders and are most often found in the 13.5% early-adopter group, although they are not exclusively located there. Opinion leaders do not know that they are such and should never be so identified. The fact is that they are sought out for a variety of reasons such as their personalities, their standing in the community, their demeanors, their longevity with the organization—any or all of these. The fact remains that they are sought out because they are respected by the seekers. They might be asked a variety of questions: Who do you like in the upcoming election? Who is going to win the Super Bowl? What do you think about management's new offer to the union? One thing will become apparent: Sooner or later, they will be asked about the new program for excellence.

If the opinion leaders in the organization can be confidently identified, management need only develop a meaningful communicational relationship with them to have a pretty good idea as to how things are going throughout the organization.

There are not a lot of opinion leaders in an organization, perhaps 5% or so of all employees. And they are not always obvious. Nor do they necessarily come from the management or supervisory levels. The person who delivers the mail to various departments could be an opinion leader, as could one of the engineers who travel to virtually every corner of the property. One of the housekeeping members will undoubtedly be an opinion leader within that group, as will be one of the waiters or waitresses in food service. Department Heads will have a pretty good idea as to who the opinion leaders are in their departments. Once you have identified opinion leaders, do not identify them publically or form them into any sort of a group. This will tend to destroy their effectiveness. Management should just be aware of their value to the overall communication process and try to interact with them as individuals regularly. Ask their advice about the Journey to Excellence program. What they will tell you is not their thinking alone but that in their circles of influence. It is important to note that their communicational value works in both incoming and outgoing directions. If they are casually informed about how the program is proceeding, this will be communicated to those with whom they interact.

A word of caution: When you explain the opinion-leader concept to others, there will always be a few who believe that the process is really a form of manipulation, and thus, undesirable. This is not so. Opinion leaders occur in social systems as a natural element, much as gravity occurs as a natural element. What management is doing is simply recognizing the fact that opinion leaders exist and plugging in to the established communication process. There must be total intellectual honesty in the communications. Remember the communicational power in the opinion-leader group. Feeding them misinformation or exaggerated claims will backfire with disastrous results once they discover the abuse and communicate it to their groups. Treat the opinion leaders with respect, and you have created a large asset to the Journey to Excellence process. Trying to manipulate and misuse the opinion leaders will destroy the program.

Opinion Leaders are very important to the communication process, thus they should be respected and treated accordingly.

MAINTAINING MOMENTUM

33

TRAINING

Training is a process of creating change in one or more of three areas: knowledge, skill, and attitude. The process consists of two steps once it is determined that change is necessary. First, the individual needs to be moved from his or her current position to the desired position. Many programs stop here. The second step is critical: The individual needs to be locked into the new desired position. The locking-in process consists of consistently monitoring and insisting that the new condition be adopted until it becomes habit. Once habit is achieved, the locking-in process can be less intense, but the monitoring process must be continuous, lest the employee gradually revert to his or her old habits. Many managers have a tendency to believe that the training process alone will bring permanent change without managements continued vigil. This deficiency defeats the training.

Once, while I was working on a project in the Bahamas, a General Manager told me, "Last year I spent $350,000 on training programs, and I have nothing to show for it." I am certain of two facts. First, he was exaggerating to make a point, and second, he was being brutally truthful regarding the ineffectiveness of many training programs. There are 4 reasons why training programs lack effectiveness. The first reason is that we often do not train the individual; rather, we train the extended ego. People tend to become what their superiors want them to become at the time change is requested. Employees at all levels will readily accept training programs during the presentation of those programs, but this does not mean that they lock into the change proposed. When the programs end, employees often revert to their old ways unless there is sufficient, strong follow-up to lock in the change. The second reason is that the hospitality industry in particular experiences tremendous turnover, sometimes as high as 50%. This constant infusion of new employees with different skills, knowledge, and attitudes means the dilution of the training unless a program is in place to integrate the new employees quickly and permanently into the newly changed organization. The third reason is that the monitoring and locking process requires skill on the part of supervisors who are often untrained in supervisory skills. Too often managers focus on the need to change the production-level employees without considering how those employees will be managed once changed. The final reason that training programs are not effective is that all standards are often not in the required clear and concise written form, as previously discussed.

An underlying fundamental of training is the fact that every employee is a trainer. The employee either does the task correctly, thus setting the proper example, or performs it incorrectly, which sets a bad example. It is the issue of right or wrong that argues strongest for the commitment of all standards to written form. We have all played the game where a spoken message is communicated from person to person around a circle. When the communication returns to the starting point, it seldom resembles the original message. The same holds true to the verbal communication of standards that are not communicated from a precise, written base. Many organizations train new employees by putting them with an old employee for a short period of time. All bad habits of the old employee are transmitted to the new employees, which results in an employee who does not perform to the required standards. Training must always take place against an absolute standard, and that standard is the written, accepted set of standards developed by the excellence program. When all employees are trained against written standards, monitored against written standards and locked in against written standards, positive habits are formed and the result of positive habits is excellence.

Let us explore briefly the role of the professional outside trainer. Many are very good at what they do and most certainly earn their fees; however, the effectiveness of their work measured in lasting changes to the employees being trained is questionable. First, unless there are precise written standards to train for, the training becomes too general. Second, training is not a one-time shot-in-the-arm quick fix; rather, it is a daily multivitamin supplement producing value over time. Effective training is an ongoing process of measuring performance against standards, and the one-time approach cannot perform this function. Professional trainers can be effective in one crucial area, training the trainers on how to conduct effective training. Again, however, written standards are critical if the training is to be successful.

**Every employee is a trainer, for better or worse,
and a complete set of published standards
is the only path to a successful training effort.**

34

MONITORING

A most relevant management saying concerning the Journey to Excellence is "You get out of people what you "***inspect***" to get. Merely telling people what you want and leaving them alone, assuming they will produce it is to embark on a fool's errand. It will not work. Without monitoring, the Journey to Excellence program will soon fail. Management needs to be constantly assured that their standards are being met, not just sporadically, but each and every time the standards are relevant. Management confidence is a function of monitoring.

The most effective monitoring is personal observation. Sam Walton, founder of Wal-Mart, called it MBA - management by walking around. By moving out of your office periodically, you can tell if the front desk lines are too long and if the cross-trained front desk personnel are in place. You can tell if the service staff in the dining rooms is serving correctly per your standards. A visit to a guest room will adequately monitor the housekeeping function, and an occasional visit to the engineering area will tell, by looking at the assignment board, whether maintenance calls are being made efficiently. And certainly, an occasional look inside the coolers and freezers and the storerooms will tell if they are being maintained according to standards. But not everything lends itself to visual inspection. You cannot visually check whether the bell staff is properly communicating to the guests while taking them to their rooms. Nor can you visually observe how the room service waiter is setting up the table and presenting the meal.

One approach to those standards that cannot be physically observed is to ask the guest to fill out a survey form. My feeling on guest survey forms is that they do not always return truthful and helpful comments. For starters, many people just don't take the time to fill them out. This is especially true for questions requiring long, thoughtful answers. The situation can be improved vastly if the relevant standard is listed with a simple "yes/no" answer about whether the standards were met, but surveys tend to make the guest the inspector in an impersonal way.

In my opinion, the best approach is to personally call a sampling of guests within minutes of them being roomed and to ask them about the standards. For example, you could ask if that bell person, on the way to the room, satisfactorily explained the services offered by the hotel (which he or she had previously been trained to do in a certain professional way). You would inquire as to whether the bell person properly explained the heating and air-conditioning controls and physically checked the bathroom to ensure that it was ready for occupancy. If the call and questioning are done properly, the guest will appreciate the personal touch. The conversation does not have to be long and intrusive to the guest and could be combined with a welcome and a "thank you" for staying with you. If you personally check in with the guests, the bell staff will know you are serious about the proper application of your standards and will, in all likelihood, treat the process more seriously. Further, by quickly gathering the information, it is possible to talk to the bell person while the process is still fresh in his or her mind.

The same kind of a call could be made following a room service delivery. Was the meal delivered in a timely manner and set up professionally according to your written standards? Was the food at the correct temperature, attractive in appearance, and cooked to the guest's instructions? Was the coffee hot, the juice cold, and the bacon crisp? Was the overall experience a satisfactory one for the guest?

Many dining room managers have the habit of stopping by the table during a meal, usually with the simple question "is everything all right?" This generally evokes a simple "everything is fine" answer. The whole conversation is simply a standard stimulus followed by a conditioned response. This really does not provide much valuable information or become relevant to either party. If you have in mind certain areas to be improved, such as long wait times to be seated, a better approach would be to be specific in your question: "Good evening, folks. Welcome to the Fireside Hearth Restaurant. I hope you are enjoying your meal and you did not have to wait long to be seated tonight?" This kind of conversation calls for a thoughtful response rather than a conditioned one, and it reinforces the standards you are implementing to solve the long-wait condition. It is a much more personal approach and comes across as you being truly interested in the guest's welfare more than the perfunctory "Is everything all right?"

The management burden is always present, but the more you know about how things really are, the lighter the burden will be.

35

A WORD ABOUT SUGGESTION BOXES

In an attempt to recognize employees and include them in the management process, many companies and organizations have implemented suggestion box programs. The belief is that no one knows the problems in an organization better than the employees, the ones closest to the issue. In most cases this is true. It is also believed that those dealing with the problem are in the best position to suggest solutions. This, unfortunately, is not true. Those best suited to implement solutions are those in management if and when the problems are identified. Further, in an attempt to encourage the suggestion box system, management frequently rewards those who make meaningful suggestions that solve the problems. In reality, some employees are very good at playing the suggestion box game and participate frequently. Others participate infrequently or not at all but that does not signify lack of interest, just lack of solutions. The philosophy of the suggestion system should not be that of receiving solutions but, rather, on identifying errors. Obviously, solutions are readily accepted and appreciated but that should not be the main focus. Once a problem area (an error) is identified, employee recognition is quickly achieved by a sincere thank you and a call for more input by that employee's supervisor as to possible solutions. Such interactions are interpersonal and effective in developing the feeling on the employee's part that they are a meaningful part of the team.

Suggestion box systems should focus on identifying errors rather than solutions in order to create effective participation

36

MEASURING RESULTS

You cannot manage what you cannot measure. This is especially true in the Journey to Excellence. Although it is absolutely true that the ultimate measurement of success is the perception of the customer, it is critical for management to continuously keep a finger on the pulse of progress. Traditionally, the measurement process takes the form of a sliding scale. Customers are asked to rate elements of the excellence program in term of "excellent, good, average, sub-standard, and unsatisfactory" or some variation thereof. This is the wrong approach to measurement. The goal of excellence must be perfection, that is, 100% compliance to published standards. Is such a condition attainable? The answer is "NO" for two reasons. First, if the goal of 100% compliance is achieved, it probably means that more-stringent standards are possible, and second, more-stringent standards possess more opportunities to occasionally fall short. A difficult goal is never an excuse for a mediocre effort, however. We used to have a saying in our family that "if you shoot for the stars and fail, you land on the moon, but if you shoot for the lamp post and fail, you end up back on the street." I am also reminded of a question that was asked of me when I was interviewed for acceptance into the Naval ROTC program at Cornell University: "Is there any limit to how high a person can pole vault?" The answer is unquestionably "Yes, there is a limit." But until many years have passed without the best jump being exceeded, the limit will not be known. And even then, jumpers will strive to go higher, whether or not it is ever possible. In other words, the human nature of winners is to always strive for perfection without considering that perfection is probably not possible. This discussion assumes, of course, that the goals are basically achievable and are not set unreasonably high.

Now to return to our point regarding the utilization of a sliding-scale rating system: What such a system really identifies is that we "averaged well." By accepting "good" to "excellent" as acceptable, we acknowledge that we are willing to accept less than our established standards, and less than perfection will be our result. The proper way to approach measurement is to determine that nothing short of 100% compliance to our published standards is acceptable and to simply measure whether each standard was met. Our standard must be a clean guest room upon check-in. An "almost clean" guest room is never acceptable. The guest room is either totally clean, or we failed to meet our standard. A guest rating room cleanliness as "good" should not make us happy even if we rate mostly excellent on the question, because although it indicates a high level of satisfaction, it still also indicates that we will lose a certain number of repeat guests because of a failure to meet our cleanliness standard.

Let me illustrate another point in the sliding-scale approach. I once worked for a hotel chain that prided itself that each year; overall occupancy went up, however slightly. Assume that one year the chain averaged 75% occupancy, versus 74% the year before. A celebration was in order. But it is possible that occupancy really increased by 3 points because we did a good job in some areas and decreased by 2 points because of a not-so-good job in other areas. The result would be a 1-point gain over the year, but if everything had been right and 2 points had not been lost, the actual gain would have been 3 points, a much greater cause for celebration. Averaging well is not acceptable. The only acceptable result is total perfection of attainable published standards.

Average companies are content to "average well," but total compliance is the only goal for companies truly seeking excellence.

37

RECOGNITION

Many properties have programs for recognizing worthy employees, but these efforts are often misguided. The idea is noteworthy, but the implementation is counterproductive. Programs generally consist of honoring the employee of the month by a photo and a write-up on the bulletin and/or in the company newsletter. Sometimes it includes lunch with the General Manager or, at least, a personal ceremony in the manager's office. The belief is that by seeing another employee recognized in such a way, all the other employees will be motivated to strive to win the honor. It seldom has this result, however.

Excellence cannot be achieved by a group of individually meritorious employees. It is a question of every employee following the published standards and being motivated to do so. Management cannot always be present to monitor employee activities; thus, very often, there are lapses in implementation of proper standards. Those who know best whether the standards are being applied properly are the employees themselves. I vividly remember a meeting of employees in a Bermuda hotel in which one employee stated, "Don't you know what Thursday is? It is supply day, and all the employees go to the storeroom to get their home supplies." Management had no clue up to that point that such a process had been taking place with their guest room supplies. In another example, this time in a four-star property in the United States, employees in the dishwashing area acknowledged that the dumbwaiter bringing dirty dishes from the floor above would often jamb, causing substantial breakage that was immediately cleaned up and "forgotten." Again, management had no clue. The point is that the employees not only know what is happening better than management but can also decide to remain silent and let the errors go uncorrected. Most often, this depends on the employees' respect for management. All of this argues for a team approach rather that an individual one.

The best approach is to recognize work teams. The employee base should be broken down into manageable small teams such as night maids, day maids (and even section maids in large properties). The front office is a team, as is the service staff in the various dining outlets. Day engineers and night engineers compose teams as do doormen, bellmen, valets, and housemen. Don't overlook the sales and marketing team and especially management. (Yes, senior management also must follow standards of excellence relevant to their contribution to the organization.) Obviously, smaller properties will have different classifications, but the concept remains valid.

Once the measurement groups are identified, the relevant standards are identified, and the measurement begins. During the month, informal inspections are conducted on the basis of meeting the standard 100%. A simple percentage attainment is calculated and provides the basis for a monthly ranking of measurement groups, forming the basis for recognition. A list, from best to last, should be posted for all employees to see, and the winning group warrants a personal visit and thank-you from management. Of course, those groups with lower scores will be visited by their department heads to discuss improvement. By approaching recognition in this manner, the organization motivates employees to check one another so as to add score to their work group. This is the result you are seeking.

Management will argue that they do not have time for such a process, but one must ask, “Why is there always enough time to do things over but never enough time to do things right the first time?” If there were no errors to correct, how much added time would management have?

There is another aspect of recognition in the Journey to Excellence program. It is a more general approach. Numerous times during interactions with employees, I ask, “If I had a magic wand and could change one thing in your working relationship with this organization, what would you want changed?” When the answers are discussed with management, management usually believes that “more money” or “less work” will be employees’ answer. Almost unanimously, however, the employee answer is “I would like management to know we exist.” Returning to our four-star resort where broken dishes were not reported, the employees’ response to what they wanted changed was “recognition.” When this finding was presented to management, the General Manager readily acknowledged that members of management do a good job of interacting with everyone they meet on the way to their office in the morning and during the daily routine but virtually never journey to the dish room or the engineering areas. A program was established to make such "off the beaten path" visits mandatory and attitudes changed immediately. It was during such a visit to the dish room that an employee asked when they might expect to see the dumbwaiter fixed so as to avoid more breakage.

There is a famous story outside the hospitality industry that further illustrates this point. It seems that a number of shipping companies utilizing rail transportation were experiencing goods arriving throughout the county in broken condition. They could not figure out why until an investigating team discovered that a Midwest switching facility had a section of track that caused cars to sway when entering the yard. High up in a platform overlooking the yard was a team of individuals responsible for reallocating freight cars to various engines leaving for sections of the country. As freight cars would pass over the uneven track, the swaying would cause freight to move and sometimes break. The employees in the switch tower had watched the swaying condition take place for 2 years and had said nothing. When asked why, they replied, "We have been asking for 2 years for a fan to remove the unbearable summer heat in that tower, and management did nothing. When management cares enough to help us, we will care enough to help them." It is not a nice story but an understandable one. The point is that recognized employees are motivated employees, and recognized employees often add enlightenment to management. Recognition is essential for the Journey to Excellence to succeed.

Proper recognition results in motivated employees and enlightened management, both of which are critically essential to the attainment of excellence.

38

RENEWAL

To recap where we are with our program, we have identified relevant job titles, and for each job title, we have further identified the relevant tasks. Then we began the process of developing standards as necessary under the various tasks. We observed that it is not necessary to develop the complete list of standards prior to implementing the Journey to Excellence program, as the philosophy is to move slowly but steadily to completion at a pace that permits total absorption of the important "need-now" standards before the addition of new ones. The process is a continuous one that never ends. The title, task, and standards documents are stored in a selected word processing program, which facilitates recall and publication of the standards at any time.

The underlying concept of renewal can be illustrated by an example taken from manufacturing. The philosophy on renewal of innovations in the automotive industry differs between U.S. and Japanese manufacturers. In America, proposed changes are collected and implemented in each model change, whereas innovations for Japanese manufacturers are incorporated as soon as possible. This means that the next car off the Japanese line is as up to date as it can be but in the U.S. buyers must wait a year or more for the latest updates. In the hospitality industry, very competitive in nature, it is important that what we present to the consuming guest is the very best we can offer at our market level for the next check-in. Jim Bennett, Manager for many years of the Boston Ritz Carleton hotel, put it this way: "In hospitality we are not judged by what we did in the past but, rather, what we do in the next 30 minutes." He was acknowledging that although situations repeat themselves over and over in hospitality, the specifics in each situation vary constantly largely because people with different personalities and different needs are involved. It is therefore crucial that improvements are applied continuously. If we want excellence, our next product or process offering must be the best we can offer.

With the system outlined in this book, it is possible to update the organization's standards at any time. This makes the Journey to Excellence alive, dynamic, and totally relevant. Whereas constant updating is a necessary, annual updating, or renewal, is a must. Annual renewal takes the form of the department head reviewing the standards with the relevant supervisor and selected production-level employees to change unworkable standards, increasing the standard where possible and/or adding new standards. Doing so has 3 major contributions to the program:

- **Employee involvement is maintained, which heightens interest.**
- **The latest and best standards are always in use.**
- **Management focus and commitment to the program are reinforced.**

Once the review has taken place, the revised standards are reentered in the computer, which now has the official "marching orders" for the entire organization. The task then becomes that of training, monitoring, measuring, and recognizing to ensure that the standards are being met consistently. A visual image that would illustrate the process might be that of the hula hoop. Although it takes some effort to learn how to make the hoop spin (some time to implement the Journey to Excellence program), once the skill is mastered, it takes little effort to keep the hoop moving.

Another benefit of renewal is the fact that once standards are mastered by the employees, pride in accomplishment grows and compliance becomes easier. Employees will suggest standards that are even more stringent. Once it is determined that new standards are attainable with proper effort, they are then enacted. For example, assume that the standard for delivering breakfast room service is 45 minutes, but having mastered that standard and with proper organization, it is felt that 30 minutes is attainable, then the standard can be improved. Or, if the standard is that no more than 4 guests should be in the morning checkout line but improved organization and effective cross training can permit a target of 3 guests in line, then the standard can be improved. A motel might determine that too much time is spent advising guests about local dining possibilities or attractions. Developing an in-room or check-in handout can significantly reduce this time, and it may well cause a check-in time standard to be revised, as calls to the front desk are reduced. Management does not bear the full burden of identifying ways to increase standards. A motivated employee will make a significant contribution.

A proper Journey to Excellence program is in a constant state of renewal.

39

CONCLUSION

There are several salient points to make in conclusion:

Without total senior management commitment, the program will not succeed.

Excellence is the inseparable union of quality and ethics.

The definition of ethics can be simplified as respecting the legal personal property of others.

Excellence is the diligent application of common sense.

The Journey to Excellence program can, and should, be done in house.

The exception to the in-house rule is using a professional "Train the Trainer" course.

It costs very little money to achieve total excellence.

Meaningful involvement of all employees is tantamount to success.

> Excellence is not a destination; it is a continuous journey.
>
> The heart of the quest for excellence process is written standards at all levels.
>
> 100% compliance in implementing standards is a mandatory goal.
>
> Excellence builds trust, which builds repeat business and increased profits.
>
> Excellence does not cost....IT PAYS!

We began our discussion of excellence by suggesting that every element of the Journey to Excellence program is based on logic. The reader should now ask whether the elements contained in this book meet the test of logic or not. If they do, it then makes sense to initiate a program of excellence. It they do not, and if the reader can point to areas based on supposition and generalization rather than common sense, I have failed in my delivery of the components. I do not believe this will be the case, however. Many years of study and application of the principles in this book have shown the logic of the approach such that it can and will work if applied diligently as set forth.

If most managers agree with the logic, why, then, is there so much confusion regarding the achievement of excellence? I believe it is due to the traditional character of the hospitality industry. Few industries have as great a gap between the required skills of the production-level and management-level employees as the hospitality industry. This has spawned a belief that employees must be told what to do and must be rigidly controlled to ensure that they do what has been dictated. That is to say, management has the attitude that employees cannot think for themselves and be self-motivating. Some chains in the 1990s and just after the turn of the century recognized this misperception and launched programs wherein employees were given great latitude to grant rebates and other perks when warranted by unmet standards. This is a classic case of trying to solve a problem by too great a quantum leap. The concept of empowering employees to make management decisions regarding compensation for failed standards did not and will not work. The concept must never be based on how to compensate the guest for our failures; rather, it must be based on how to guarantee that failures do not occur in the first place.

At this point, management will write off this premise on the basis that "mistakes are inevitable" and cannot be avoided. This attitude is self-defeating. As long as errors are tolerated as not preventable, that is exactly what will result—"unpreventable" errors. The level of respect that hospitality managers have for production-level employees must be improved. Perhaps this idea will help establish a new direction in employee perception. I was once told, "Respect those who are doing jobs you would not like to do, lest they become yours." The maid is on her hands and knees, cleaning the floor of the bathroom. Perhaps the guest's celebration the previous night was a bit messy, but the maid is expected to return the room to pristine condition. Of course, that is a job management would not like. Be nice to the maid. Shortly after I began work in a major hotel chain, we had a strike, and I was sent, along with many others, to the property to fill in during the negotiations. One of my tasks was to hose out the sewer sump tank, not a pleasant task. I developed a very strong appreciation for the engineering department right then and there! Employees quickly sense when the perception of management is that they are second-class citizens. They also sense, however, when they are viewed as making meaningful contributions. Treat others as if they can meet your expectations, and chances are, they will. This is an important attitude to carry into the Journey to Excellence program.

My goal was to produce a book on excellence with factual, easy-to-absorb principles that can be effectively applied with meaningful results. Hopefully, I have succeeded, and you will soon be on your way to a new level of excellence. Enjoy the journey.

Bon Voyage

40

A JOURNEY TO EXCELLENCE IMPLEMENTATION CHECK LIST

In a general way the following list presents the steps necessary to implement the Journey to Excellence program outlined in this book. They are presented in linear form but, quite obviously, it is not intended to say or imply that any step must be completed before the succeeding step in begun. Journey to Excellence is a process, a journey, rather than a destination. The process develops its own energy if carefully implemented.

1 The most senior executive decides to commit to the Journey to Excellence concept
2 The senior management team is asked to commit
3 If a chain property, the headquarters team is asked to commit to the process
4 A Journey to Excellence Director is identified and assigned

5 A 3 to 5 person Journey to Excellence (JTE) committee is identified and assigned

6 A meeting of supervisors and department heads is called to present and discuss the JTE program

7 The JTE committee establishes a one hour weekly meeting time. The JTE secretary is identified

8 The JTE committee begins reviewing job titles (Include department heads and supervisors)

9 Management identifies opinion leaders and informally presents the program

10 Management discusses the JTE program with the union if one is involved

11 The fine tuned job title list is accepted by management and set up in a word processing program

12 Working with department heads and supervisors, the committee begins identifying job title tasks

13 Supervisors and department heads begin to identify major areas where improvement is needed

14 Cost of error calculations are done on selected errors to show the cost impact

15 Slowly standards are created and implemented to correct areas of needed improvement

16 Each standard is tested for ethical impact and monitoring capability

17 As tasks and standards are created they are entered into the word processing program

18 Training is set up where required as identified by the JTE committee

19 Department heads and supervisors identify and recognize those who are meeting quality standards

20 Work teams are identified and monitoring processes established

21	Throughout the JTE process management and the JTE committee check with opinion leaders
22	High performing JTE work teams are identified and recognized for good performance
23	Throughout the JTE process information regarding progress is communicated to all employees
24	A "suggestion" box is established for employees requesting that they identify errors to be corrected
25	At the end of the year, each supervisor is give his/her list of standards to review and fine tune

41

SUMMARY RECAP OF PRINCIPLES

1	THE JOURNEY BEGINS	Every element of the process of achieving excellence can be defended by the application of logic
2	DEFINING QUALITY	Quality is commonly defined as "Conformance to standards."
3	QUALITY AT EVERY LEVEL	Quality applies to every market level from low end to luxury
4	DEFINITION OF STANDARD	Standards are required levels of performance
5	CHARACTERIS-TICS OF A STANDARD	Standards are attainable, clear, concise, in writing and measurable levels of required performance
6	THE COST OF ERROR	An error is a standard not met and every error is costly.
7	WHAT ABOUT EXCELLENCE?	Excellence is the inseparable union of quality (consistency) and ethics (doing right things)
8	A LOOK AT SIX SIGMA	Although a Six Sigma performance may not be practical for Hospital-ity, the goal of zero errors remains relevant.

9	THE BLACK SWAN EVENT	The consequences of a black swan event make the prevention of errors a crucial concern.
10	WHAT IT MEANS TO BE ETHICAL	Ethics is "knowing what is right and having the will to do it."
11	THE NEED FOR A SIMPLIFIED BASE FOR ETHICS	The subject of ethics is important to hoteliers but is made difficult by becoming too complicated.
12	INTRODUCING A SIMPLIFIED BASIS FOR ETHICS	A simple way of viewing ethics is that it is based on the right of a person or entity to control property that is legally owned
13	ANOTHER ASPECT OF ETHICS	Increasing the value of the property of others is also an ethical act.
14	7 BASIC TESTS FOR ETHICAL DECISIONS	Acting ethically, a journey not a destination, requires that every decision be carefully evaluated from many perspectives.
15	IS MY DECISION LEGAL	"Is my decision legal?" is an excellent first test but not absolute in helping us decide what is ethical.
16	WILL MY DECISION HURT ANYONE?	Often decisions unavoidably hurt others but an ethical path will do everything possible to minimize the hurt.
17	IS MY DECISION FAIR?	Fairness, although often a thin line, is, nevertheless, a valid test for ethical decisions.

18	AM I BEING HONEST WITH MY DECISION?	It is never right to be dishonest but there are times when it may be more ethical to withhold the truth than to speak it.
19	CAN I LIVE WITH MY DECISION?	Our conscience that dictates whether or not we can live with an ethical decision is a personal choice and is difficult to apply to the choices of others except as a personal opinion.
20	WOULD I ANNOUNCE MY DECISION PUBLICALLY?	If it is important that others not know what you are doing, it might be an indication that what you are doing is wrong.
21	WHAT IF EVERY-BODY DID IT?	If what you are deciding would not work as a universal decision it has a high probability of being unethical.
22	AN OVERVIEW OF VANESSA	Ignoring small non-threatening ethical dilemmas often leads to being confronted with major difficult ones
23	THE VALUE OF ETHICS	Placing the customer first and practicing ethics at every level of the organization will pay great dividends for the company.
24	EXAMPLES OF ETHICAL ISSUES	The Hospitality Industry needs to increase its focus on ethical issues in order to maintain consumer trust.
25	WRITING A CODE OF EXCELLENCE	A meaningful code of ethics is the moral compass of the organization and the individuals therein.

26	ASSEMBLING THE TEAM	A successful Program for Excellence results from a committed top management working through a qualified Director who supervises and motivates a dedicated Committee.
27	STARTING THE JOURNEY TO EXCELLENCE	A successful Program for Excellence is a slow, deliberative process of constant improvement allowing employees to absorb standards and implement them to perfection with total consistency.
28	HANDLING THE A-TYPICAL STANDARD	A-typical standards are best handled by one standard directing the subject to a broader training process.
29	WORKING WITH THE UNION	Bringing the union on board early on is a necessary step in a successful Journey to Excellence program.
30	DIFFUSION - A HELPFUL TOOL	Excellence is an idea perceived by many to be new; understanding the principles of adoption facilitates the process of implementation.
31	ADOPTER CATEGORIES AND THE PROCESS	Individuals adopt new ideas in predictable ways which, when understood, facilitates the adoption process.
32	OPINION LEADERS	Opinion Leaders are very important to the communicational process if respected and treated accordingly.

33	TRAINING	Every employee is a trainer for better or worse and a complete set of published standards is the only path to a successful training effort.
34	MONITORING	The management burden is always present but, the more you know about how things really are, the lighter the burden will be.
35	A WORD ABOUT SUGGESTION BOXES	Suggestion box systems should focus on identifying errors rather than solutions in order to create effective participation
36	MEASURING	Average companies are content to "average well" but total compliance is the only goal for companies on a Journey to Excellence.
27	RECOGNITION	Proper recognition results in motivated employees and enlightened management both critically essential to the attainment of excellence
38	RENEWAL	A proper Journey to Excellence program is in a constant state of renewal.

LaVergne, TN USA
27 October 2010
202537LV00001B/5/P